INVISIBLE VICTIMS

Missing and Murdered Indigenous Women

by Katherine McCarthy

CRIMES CANADA:
True Crimes That Shocked The Nation
~ Volume 15~

Katherine McCarthy

INVISIBLE VICTIMS
Missing and Murdered Indigenous Women

by Katherine McCarthy

CRIMES CANADA:
True Crimes That Shocked The Nation
~ Volume 15~

www.CrimesCanada.com

ISBN-13: 978-1534754607
ISBN-10: 1534754601

Copyright and Published (2016)
VP Publications an imprint of
RJ Parker Publishing, Inc.
Published in Canada

Invisible Victims

Copyrights

This book is licensed for your personal enjoyment only. All rights reserved. No part of this publication can be reproduced or transmitted in any form or by any means without prior written authorization from Peter Vronsky or RJ Parker of VP Publications and **RJ Parker Publishing, Inc**. The unauthorized reproduction or distribution of a copyrighted work is illegal. Criminal copyright infringement, including infringement without monetary gain, is investigated by the FBI and is punishable by fines and federal imprisonment.

This is a work of nonfiction. No names have been changed, no characters invented, no events fabricated.

Kindle Unlimited

Enjoy these top-rated true crime eBooks from VP Publications **FREE** as part of your Kindle Unlimited subscription. You can read it on your Kindle Fire, on a computer via Kindle Cloud Reader or on any smartphone with the free Kindle reading app.

OR

Click 'Buy' and own your copy.

View All Books by RJ Parker Publishing at the following Amazon Links:

Amazon Kindle - USA

Amazon Kindle - Canada

Amazon Kindle - UK

Amazon Kindle - Australia

View Crimes Canada Book at:
rjpp.ca/CC-CRIMES-CANADA-BOOKS

Invisible Victims

Dedication

This book is dedicated to all the missing and murdered indigenous women and girls in Canada. To the missing, may it be that you find your way home safely. To those who have died violently, may it be that you find justice. To all their families and loved ones, may it be that you find peace.

Msit No'kmaq/All my relations

Katherine McCarthy

Table of Contents

Series Introduction..9
Preface..11
Introduction: Violence Towards Indigenous Women. 19
Number of MMIW..27
Root Causes..39
    The Indian Act...47
    Residential Schools..57
    The Sixties Scoop...61
    Forced Sterilizations & Eugenics.....................65
    Role of DNA..71
MMIW Crimes..73
    Carol Nora King (SK).....................................73
    Toronto's Sisters of Spirit................................87
    Highway of Tears (British Columbia)............101
        Victims and Suspects..................................106
    Anna Mae Pictou (NS & USA).......................119
Serial Killers..135
    Cody Alan Legebekoff....................................137
    Robert Pickton...147
    Gilbert Paul Jordan.......................................156
    John Martin Crawford...................................164
    Bobby Fowler...176
Conclusion...179
Acknowledgments...183
Crimes Canada Collection................................185
About The Author...187
Sources...189

Invisible Victims

Katherine McCarthy

Series Introduction

Crimes Canada: True Crimes that Shocked the Nation, will feature a series of Canadian true crime books published by VP Publication (Vronsky & Parker), an imprint of *RJ Parker Publishing, Inc.*, one of the world's leading Indie publishers of true crime.

Peter Vronsky is the bestselling author of *Serial Killers: The Method and Madness of Monsters and Female Serial Killers: How and Why Women Become Monsters* while R.J. Parker is not only a successful Indie publisher but also the author of books like *Marc Lepine: The Montreal Massacre, Serial Killers Abridged: An Encyclopedia of 100 Serial Killers, Parents Who Killed Their Children: Filicide*, and *Radical Islamic Terrorism In America Today*. Both are Canadians and have teamed up to share shocking Canadian true crime cases not only with fellow Canadian readers but with Americans and world readers as well, who will be shocked and horrified by just how evil and sick "nice" Canadians can be when they go bad.

Finally, the editors invite their established Canadian fellow authors and aspiring authors to submit proposals or manuscripts to VP Publications at *Agent@RJParkerPublishing.com*.

VP Publications is a new frontier Indie publisher, offering their published authors a generous royalty agreement payable within three months of publishing and aggressive online marketing support. Unlike many so-called "publishers" that are nothing but vanity presses in disguise, VP Publications does not charge authors in advance for submitting their proposal or manuscripts, nor do we charge authors if we choose to publish their works. We pay you, and pay well.

View the books published thus far at:

www.CRIMESCANADA.ca

Katherine McCarthy

Preface

Poison comes in many forms. For the Indigenous women of Canada, it comes in the form of disproportionate rates of violence, racism and discrimination. In recent months, one has only to turn on the news, open Facebook or Twitter to see or hear about the national crisis, Murdered and Missing Indigenous Women (MMIW) of Canada, or the fact that Indigenous women and girls are at a higher risk of being victims of violence than non-Indigenous women. However, this was not always the case. For several decades, it was Canada's dirty little secret. On the world stage, Canada has always touted itself as an open-minded country that celebrates diversity and multiculturalism. It has always been viewed as one of the most culturally tolerant countries in the world, with the friendliest and nicest people. Yet in reality, Canada has a worse racism problem than many countries. It's just harder to see.

The day I heard about the murder of Loretta Saunders, an Inuk woman from Labrador, was the day I became aware of the

Invisible Victims

MMIW crisis in Canada. The news reports spoke of her pursuing a Master's degree in Social Work from St. Mary's University in Halifax and that she was writing her thesis on this crisis. I remember a momentary confusion wondering what the MMIW crisis was all about and why was I not aware of it. Was it a large enough problem that someone was writing a thesis paper on it? And if it was indeed a 'crisis', why was it not plastered over the news for all Canadians to hear about? After all, women and girls were disappearing in this country. Women should be aware of it so they could take the necessary precautions. Law enforcement should be advising the public to be careful. I struggled to get my head around the fact that there was little to no mention of this crisis in the mainstream media.

That was the day I began my research into MMIW and also the day that the love and pride I felt for my country began to splinter. Words that never before crossed my lips are now common speak - systemic racism, marginalization, colonialism, inter-generational trauma, to list a few. Words that are so inherently frightening they shouldn't have to be used very often, let alone every day. Up to that point, I was always proud to be a Canadian. Maybe a little pompous even for being from such a great country that didn't have the same social problems that plague other countries. But now after my research for this book, I realize Canada too has significant societal issues.

Violence against women is at a breaking point. Our society is at a breaking point. Crimes against Indigenous women and girls are all too real and are happening every day. Our news is filled with inconceivable violent acts towards women. This book seeks to shine a spotlight on Canada's national MMIW crisis. With the aid of specific MMIW cases, I'll attempt to demonstrate how Indigenous women have become so devalued in society that neither the media, law enforcement, or society in general is even noticing that Indigenous women have become the most victimized group in Canada. While every single MMIW case is deserving of its own book, sadly I could only select a few to discuss here.

This work also delves into the root causes of this crisis through discussions of the various policies and programs initiated in Canada that have sought to marginalize, disassociate and assimilate Indigenous people in Canada – each one a crime against humanity in and of itself. For centuries, bureaucrats have been open and honest about their intentions to "kill the Indian in the child" and to "eliminate the Indian problem." And, yes, those phrases are in quotations because someone actually said them. Duncan Campbell Scott, the first Deputy of Indian Affairs in Canada, heartlessly uttered both in parliament meetings. I don't believe the general public is aware of just how far those bureaucrats went to achieve those goals. I would hope they would be outraged if they did know. It is also my belief that the main reason for such policies was to reduce the number of those to whom the federal government has obligations and to gain access to lands and resources. Our government needs to be held accountable for the genocidal policies and practices it has imposed on our Indigenous people for far too long.

This book is in no way an attempt to guilt non-Indigenous people. Rather it is a way to educate and inform readers about how much the Indigenous people, women specifically, have lost. It's my way to help bring awareness and hopefully some understanding and compassion to the MMIW crisis.

Some will say that it all happened ages ago and it's time to 'get over it.' Yet sadly, it wasn't that long ago that these programs designed with genocide in mind were in place. The last residential school didn't close its doors until 1996. That was the year I graduated from the university. More information about the residential school system and some of the other programs will be discussed later in the book; however, I just want to mention here that the effects of those systems are multi-generational and will take generations more to fix. Today, Indigenous children are still abused under provincial Child Protective Services programs, and Indigenous women are still going missing and are violently murdered at astronomical rates.

    Most importantly, my intention with writing this book is to help my Indigenous sisters and brothers to heal. We all know grief. And we all know far too well that healing only begins through talking. Problems like this do not begin to be resolved until enough people are talking about it and it reaches a breaking point. I believe the 2014 murder of Loretta Saunders mentioned above and the cold-blooded murder of 15-year-old Tina Fontaine in Manitoba was that breaking point. Their horrific murders made headlines, ignited widespread outrage across Canada, and finally brought this crisis to the general public's eyes and ears.

    With the new Liberal government elected in late 2015, one of the first actions initiated by our new Prime Minister, Justin Trudeau, was to commit to undertake a national inquiry into MMIW of Canada. Government officials have met with many families of the victims across Canada to get their input into the design of the inquiry. While not ideally initiated, the government has done what it said it was going to do, and hopes are high that we will get some answers and good recommendations for a solution. The national inquiry, if done correctly, should expose all of Canada's dark secrets relating to this tragedy.

When asked by my publisher to list what I considered the most shocking true crimes in Canada for this series, my number one on the list was the MMIW crisis. It honored me to be asked to write it. Throughout my writing of this book, I have tried to remain as neutral as possible. However, being a female of Mi'kmaq descent, I would be less than honest if I didn't admit to at times failing to remain completely objective – especially if discussing particularly brutal deaths or the apathy of our law enforcement and media. These women and girls are real people that are being murdered and are going missing, and not just numbers or cases.

Finally, there are various terms used all over the world when discussing Indigenous peoples. In Canada, the proper term is "Indigenous" and I will try and stick to that one as much as possible. Although you may see "Aboriginal" or "First Nations" as well, for my purposes, they mean the same thing. The term

"Indian" will only be used if it's a direct quote. Also, in Canada, the term for Indigenous communities is "reserve", whereas in the US, the term commonly used is "reservation." These both have the same meaning.

Invisible Victims

Katherine McCarthy

Introduction: Violence Towards Indigenous Women

Violence against women in Canada is becoming more and more common. Violence against Indigenous women specifically is escalating at alarming rates as is the intensity. This violence is insidiously built into the very way we think about women. It has been present for many centuries now and is deeply rooted in our psyche. The harsh truth is that being an Indigenous female in Canada means you're at risk.

Exactly how much risk are we talking about? Often violent crimes go unreported, so that risk is almost impossible to quantify with 100 percent accuracy. However, looking to Canada's homicide rate for an approximation, which by its nature is regularly reported, tracked, and used as the indicator to gauge the level of violence in society, the latest numbers indicated that even though Indigenous women only made up 4 percent of the Canadian female population, between the years 1980 and 2012, a staggering 16 percent of the women murdered in Canada were Indigenous.[1] This is a disproportionate number obviously. Also, Indigenous women are six times more likely to die a violent death than non-Indigenous women and, as *The Globe and Mail* recently reported, they are seven times more likely to be killed by serial killers.[2] That level of violence is escalating every year. However, this is true only in the case of Canada's Indigenous population. Overall murder rates in Canada are dropping[3] and our national police force, the Royal Canadian Mounted Police (RCMP), report that violent crime rates are at their lowest point since 1969.[4] Yet, in 2014, Indigenous women accounted for 21 percent of all female victims of homicide, up from 14 percent in 1991. In the case of reported sexual assaults, it is estimated that Indigenous women are victims three times that of non-Indigenous women.

So why is the level of violence towards Indigenous women increasing to these crisis levels? There is no easy answer to this question. Problems as extensive as this one are multi-dimensional, extremely complex and span centuries in its manifestation. Organizations advocating Indigenous women's rights, such as the Native Women's Association of Canada (NWAC), and other grassroots organizations have been asking the government for decades to conduct a national inquiry into why so many of our Indigenous women go missing and murdered. Previous governments have refused. Canada's former Prime Minister, Stephen Harper, even went so far as to publicly admit the crisis was "not really high on the radar"[5] even though he later tried to deny he said it. Myriad reports and recommendations have been written by human rights advocates within Canada and even internationally. Besides the ones within Canada, reports written by Amnesty International[6] in 2004, United Nations[7] in 2012, Human Right Watch[8] in 2013, and the Inter-American Commission on Human Rights[9] in 2014 strongly advised the Canadian government to fix this growing problem. The report from the Human Rights Watch made this staggering statement: "If women and girls in the general Canadian population had gone missing or been murdered at the same rate, NWAC estimates the country would have lost 18,000 Canadian women and girls since the late 1970s."[10] There is no doubt that if 18,000 Canadian women went missing, it would have been high on our previous government's radar and all over the mainstream media.

Some of these reports identified some root causes for the alarming level of violence against women. In our history books, we all learned a little about the slaughter of the

Indigenous peoples here in Canada and the US to make way for European settlers. While the slaughtering or 'physical' genocide ceased in the 1800s, the Canadian government's policies and programs implemented afterward still had genocide in mind. They were just more subtle. The Indian Act, residential schools, Sixties Scoop, forced sterilization, the pass system and many more policies were all tactics used to subdue, control and marginalize Indigenous people. Some argue the programs and policies were more akin to a 'cultural genocide' rather than the more blatant physical genocide. Whatever we call it, sad thing was, society was fine with it. When Duncan Campbell Scott stated to the House of Commons in 1920 "I want to get rid of the Indian Problem,"[11] no-one objected.

Why is it that society in general, law enforcement and the media have such a hard time seeing Indigenous women as real people? If they go missing, they aren't taken seriously. Their murder cases go unsolved for years. If they are solved, the women and girls are often portrayed poorly at trials and in the media. During the murder trial of Edmonton's Cindy Gladue, her actual preserved vagina with an 11-centimeter wound was presented as evidence.[12] Cindy, a mother of three, was found bleeding to death in a hotel bathtub. Imagine what her family went through during the trial. It was bad enough listening to details of their loved one's horrible last moments, but how humiliating it must have been to see her actual vagina paraded around the courtroom for all to see. Was that really necessary to win that case? I can't help but wonder if Cindy were an accountant or banker instead of a sex trade worker, would the prosecutor have used the same strategy? Despite the degrading act of presenting her most private body part as evidence in court, in the end, the man who made that 11-centimeter-long wound was found not guilty. I wonder if the strategy to reduce her from a human being to just a body part actually hurt their case rather than help it.

Last year, neither the artist nor the New Brunswick Heritage Days festival committee thought this painting depicting bound and gagged Mi'kmaq women, torn from their families, waiting to be raped and murdered by pirates on Phantom Ships, resigned to their fate, would upset anyone.[13] The Bathurst Council was shocked to receive a scathing letter from Patty Musgrave, host of the annual Sisters in Spirit vigil in Moncton. Their indignant response included a link to the legend of the Phantom Ships for Patty and the Mi'kmaq people to learn about their own history. As if they didn't already know it. To add insult to

Invisible Victims

injury, the painting was displayed in the window of a building where an unsolved murder of two people occurred, one a woman.

During my research, I couldn't help but notice the difference between how murdered/missing Indigenous women are reported in the media as opposed to that of non-Indigenous females. Kristin Gilchrist noticed them, too, and she conducted an actual study to explore these differences.[14] In *Newsworthy Victims,* she studied six cases - three Indigenous women and three non-Indigenous women. All were around the same age, all disappeared between 2003 and 2005. All were attending school, working and had strong family connections. None were believed to be working in the sex trade or runaways. Her study concluded that the non-Indigenous women were mentioned in the media six times more often than their Indigenous counterparts while missing. She also concluded that the word count on each article about the Indigenous women was less, the words used in headlines and the articles were more generic, less personal and lacked depth, and the actual placement of their missing person ad and articles were in a less prominent area or smaller in size than that of non-Indigenous women.

Above we discussed some of the statistics associated with violence against Indigenous women. Next let's look at the actual

Invisible Victims

number of missing and murdered women and girls.

Katherine McCarthy

Number of MMIW

In 2002, out of sheer frustration from a lack of concern or government engagement in dealing with this crisis, Native Women's Association of Canada (NWAC) and various Human Rights groups ramped up their efforts by publishing actual statistics from their own databases they were maintaining on the number of women and girls that were going missing and found murdered. From their initial report in 2002, they stated the number was around 500. They also pointed the finger at the media and law enforcement for not doing their job. Rightfully so. Interestingly, the Canadian government's own statistic from Indigenous and Northern Affairs Canada (INAC), a government-run agency, is included in that report. They knew back in 1996 that Indigenous women were five times more likely to experience a violent death. In recent years, that number has increased to six times more likely. *"Aboriginal women have been continuously reported missing across Canada. Approximately 500 Aboriginal women have been murdered or reported missing over the past 15 years. There has been little, if any, media coverage, and police do not seem to be actively searching for any of these women. Many Aboriginal women have also been murdered with no complete investigations into their deaths. We cannot forget that these women's spirits are still wandering and have not been able to rest. In 1996 Indian and Northern Affairs Canada reported that Aboriginal women with status under the Indian Act and who are between the ages of 25 and 44 are five times more likely to experience a violent death than other Canadian women in the same age category. (Aboriginal Women: A Demographic, Social and Economic Profile, Indian and Northern Affairs Canada, Summer 1996). The crime has not stopped and with approximately 1.5 million Aboriginal people in Canada and half of that population being women, Aboriginal women have become prime targets and are the most vulnerable to such acts of violence."*[15]

So these numbers and statistics that are just now gobsmacking the general public have been known for decades by the government and law enforcement.

In March 2010, NWAC concluded a five-year comprehensive study funded by a government department, Status of Women, which included the development of a database to track MMIW cases, and produced their findings. The report caused quite an upset among law enforcement and government officials. For the first time with evidence-based proof of data, indisputable connections and conclusions were made about the disproportion between Indigenous women who were victims of crime and non-Indigenous women. Ten percent of Indigenous females were victims of murder, yet they only made up 3 percent of the female population. But what really put law enforcement on the hot seat is that the study looked at not just the victim but the perpetrators of the crimes as well. They were the first to conclude that Indigenous women were more likely to be killed by a stranger than an intimate partner, and also that Indigenous women were more likely to be killed by a stranger than non-Indigenous women. They also noted that half of the cases remained unsolved, and of the ones that were solved, 40 percent of those resulted in no charges being laid. They also pinpointed geographically where the victims were being targeted - in western Canada. Seventy percent of women and girls disappeared from an urban area and 60 percent were murdered in an urban area.

The end result of all this incredible and diligent work – they were defunded and the database taken away and given to the RCMP to manage. The database would be expanded to include all missing people in Canada and would no longer just include MMIWs. NWAC was instructed by government to stop collecting data and using government funds for research or to advocate. So much for Canada's attempt to fix the MMIW crisis. Maybe this should not have been all that surprising given a few years prior to this, Canada was one of only four countries that refused to sign the UN Declaration of the Rights of Indigenous People.

Word was getting out and public pressure from Canadian citizens, and international notice of Canada's apathy forced Ottawa to dig a bit deeper into this crisis. The reports from the global watchdog Human Rights Watch, UN and Amnesty International didn't make things easy for the Harper government. Ottawa still wouldn't agree to funding a national inquiry; however, the RCMP did look at their data and, in 2014, released its findings.[16] The shock waves are still felt throughout the country.

Using data generated from Stats Canada's Homicide Survey and the shared national police database Canadian Police Information Center (CPIC) system, for the period from 1980 to 2012, the RCMP's report cited 1,181 MMIWs (164 missing and 1,017 murdered) with 225 unsolved or 20 percent.

This is a far cry from what NWAC reported at 50 percent. They also touted a 90 percent solve rate in homicide cases, which is the same for non-Indigenous women. They agreed that Indigenous women were over-represented when compared to all of Canada's missing and murdered women. However, they also were quick to argue that the perpetrators were known to the victim 90 percent of the time in an attempt to tie the issue down to one of family violence. In 2015, it released an update adding 32 more homicide cases to the list and 10 more missing women. The solve rate increased slightly to 81 percent from 80 percent, and again the report repeatedly emphasized that the victims knew their killer and that they were most often killed in their homes or communities.[17]

All that said, the RCMP was heavily motivated to point the finger at family violence as the root cause of these murders, which would be on a par with other female homicides, and it also avoided any accusation of racism on their part. When questioned about the ethnicity of the perpetrators, the RCMP would not divulge that information, saying that it was not relevant to their investigations. In their opinion, more relevant was the relationship between the victim and the perpetrator. However, in March 2015, Canada's then

Minister of Aboriginal Affairs, the very controversial Bernard Valcourt, blurted out in a closed-door meeting with First Nations chiefs that 70 percent of the perpetrators were Indigenous men and that the problem all came down to a lack of respect from men towards the women living on reserves.[18] Even though the RCMP later backed up Valcourt's revelation as true, it instantly came under intense scrutiny and no-one believed it.

With respect to the Offender-to-Victim relationship, the RCMP's breakdown revealed that 51 percent were related, 10 percent other intimate, 30 percent were acquaintances, 8 percent strangers and 1 percent unknown. So basically, the RCMP is saying that only 9 percent of murdered Indigenous women are killed by someone unknown to them. After mass outcry from the Indigenous communities, various news agencies in Canada started compiling their own data from news reports to check these numbers. Toronto's newspaper *The Star* created their own database of MMIWs based on publicly available information and from interviews. They studied 750 murder cases involving Indigenous women. Of those, 224 remain unsolved. They ended up with 420 cases where details of the relationship between victim and offender were known. Half of those were domestically related to the perpetrator, 16 percent were acquaintances, 15 percent were strangers and 13 percent were serial killers.[19] *The Globe and Mail* and *Canadian Broadcasting Corporation* are also conducting a similar comparison.

Invisible Victims

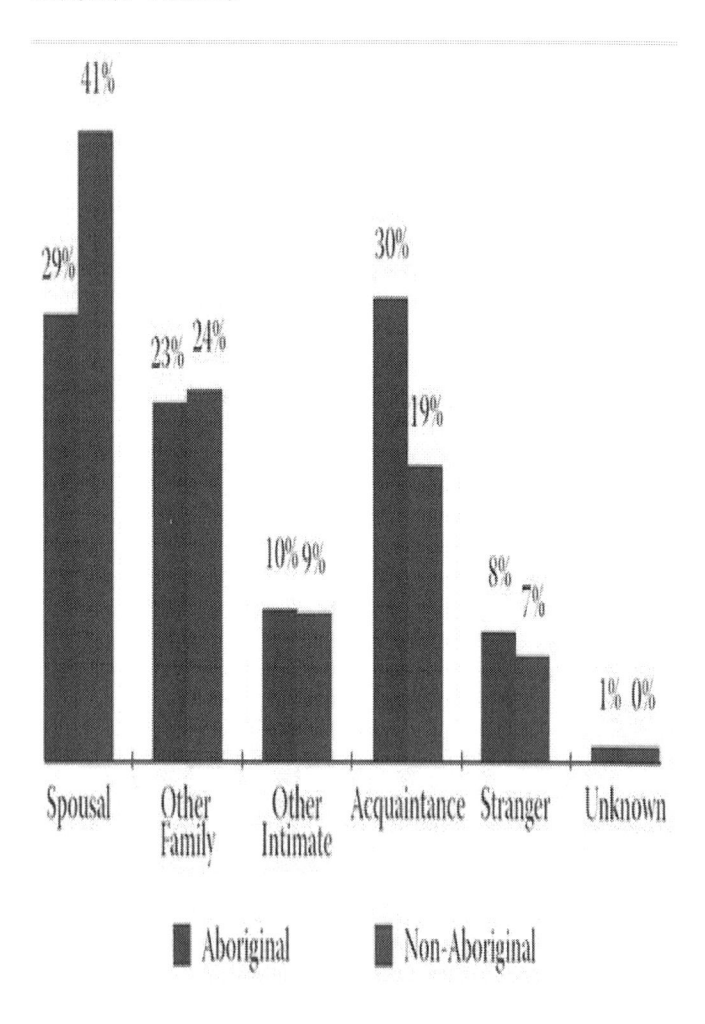

Category	Aboriginal	Non-Aboriginal
Spousal	29%	41%
Other Family	23%	24%
Other Intimate	10%	9%
Acquaintance	30%	19%
Stranger	8%	7%
Unknown	1%	0%

The RCMP report left lots of questions and doubts about its accuracy. Because it based its numbers on the Homicide Survey, it only included cases where they were sure a homicide occurred. Deaths listed by agencies as 'suspicious' or accidental were not included. There are instances where the families of Indigenous women have come forward arguing that their loved one's death was incorrectly ruled as an accidental death. In other cases they are ruled suspicious but not an actual homicide. None of those cases would be included in the RCMP's report. Also, if the RCMP failed to capture whether or not a missing woman or girl was Indigenous, then it wouldn't be in the report. They did feel strongly that the identity of any murder victims was captured correctly; however, they did admit to that potential shortcoming with respect to missing women. That said, there were also cases where a victim's family purposely omitted the fact that their loved one was Indigenous. Past bad experiences with law enforcement has led to much distrust, and a family might feel that leaving out the fact that a missing teenage girl is Indigenous might get police to take the case more seriously.

As well, some questioned the accuracy of the CPIC system itself. It had been pointed out that there was at least a two-year backlog for the data getting entered into the system with some files never making it in.[20] The RCMP's follow-up report in 2015, which added 42 more

Invisible Victims

cases, also revealed that the new additions only included data from the RCMP. No data from the other police agencies in Canada was collected for this update. There are over 300 non-RCMP agencies that are not included in this update.[21] Since Ontario and Quebec have their own police forces and do not contract out to the RCMP, no update from either of those provinces was included. Ontario and Quebec both have significant Indigenous populations. Actually, Ontario has the highest in Canada with 21.5 percent[22] of the 1.4 million Indigenous people in Canada. Quebec has another 10 percent. So there's a lot of missing cases and data from that 2015 update.

And finally, the definition of 'acquaintance' used in the RCMP report is much too broad. It encompasses all sorts of relationships from best friends to someone they may have met only once. That number would have to be broken down further to be meaningful.

So at the end of the day, no-one knows the exact number . . . yet. After concluding the discussions with MMIW family members, Indigenous Affairs Minister Carolyn Bennett said, "It's bigger than 1,200; way, way bigger than 1,200." Many grassroots organizations say they estimate the number is closer to 4,000.

Hopefully, the national inquiry will remedy that. Regardless, one is too many.

Invisible Victims

Katherine McCarthy

Root Causes
Indigenous Women History

In order to understand how the Indigenous people, especially the women, have become so marginalized in Canadian society, we have to look to our history. Prior to European contact, the lives of Indigenous women were drastically different than what they became afterwards. Many Indigenous societies were matrilineal or egalitarian, as opposed to the patriarchal structure of the Europeans who were settling in North America. Indigenous women played a vital role in the survival and governance of the community and in all aspects of spiritual life. They were held in the highest esteem. Revered, even, for their spiritual and mental strength. A division of labor existed; however, this did not mean one type or the other was inferior. All jobs were equally valued and also flexible. Everyone had their roles based on their strengths. The men were usually responsible for providing food, shelter and clothing. Women, as the life-givers, were responsible for all things domestic and child rearing. This usually included the management of the community resources and all matters impacting social life and government. They controlled the resources for the community, made or at least had an equal say in all strategical decisions that impacted the community, including decisions about warfare. Clan Mothers usually held a higher leadership position than Chief. They decided who became chief and could remove him from that position as well. "Traditional Indigenous society experienced very little family breakdown. Husbands and wives were expected to respect and honor one another and to care for one another with honesty and kindness. In matriarchal societies, such as the Mohawk, women were honored for their wisdom and vision. Aboriginal men also respected women for the sacred gifts which they believed the Creator had given to them."[23]

In the teachings passed down through generations, many Indigenous nations' men and women were truly equal in power and autonomy. "Women figured centrally in almost all Aboriginal creation legends. In Ojibwa and Cree legends, it was a woman who came to earth through a hole in the sky to care for the earth. It was a woman, Nokomis (grandmother), who taught Original Man (Anishinabe, an Ojibwa word meaning "human being") about the medicines of the earth and about technology. When a traditional Ojibwa person prays, thanks is given and the pipe is raised in each of the four directions, then to Mother Earth, as well as to Grandfather, Mishomis, in the sky. To the Ojibwa, the earth is woman, the Mother of the people, and her hair, the sweetgrass, is braided and used in ceremonies. The Dakota and Lakota (Sioux) people of Manitoba tell how a woman – White Buffalo Calf Woman -- brought the pipe to their people. It is through the pipe that prayer is carried by its smoke upwards to the Creator in their most sacred ceremonies."[24]

Oral history and wampum belts (the method used by Indigenous people to record events) depict intentions of peace and sharing in the early days of contact with Europeans. The Indigenous people of Canada helped the visiting Europeans survive in the sometimes cruel climate, and often showed them the best river systems and trade routes, thereby creating strong friendships that the Indigenous people took seriously. Things were very different before the European powers set sights on North and South America as a way to expand their empires.

Once the Spanish and Portuguese conquered the Indigenous people of South and Central America, it made way for other

European powers -- France and Britain. It marked the beginning of the creation of a European-dominated economy. It also unleashed an unceasing wave of migration, trade, conquest and colonization.[25] The presence of Indigenous people blocked the way for settlers; however, that was easily remedied through treaties, or the imposition of new political systems, or if worse came to worst, wars of extinction. The outcome for Indigenous people was disastrous.

In later centuries, Europeans arrived in mass numbers. Lured by promises of free land and a brand new start, away from the centuries-old bickering, British, Scottish, Irish, French and German, to name a few, migrated to Canada. It wasn't long, though, before their European wars and feuds followed. Their Indigenous friends were called on to help fight, and mutually beneficial treaties were signed.

Katherine McCarthy

The various wars among the British, French and Spanish resulted in the death of many Indigenous people. Disease that followed these wars wiped out many more. After the wars were over and more and more Europeans moved to Canada to live, the victors needed land for them. And in typical European style of conquer and defeat, previous friendships and treaties were tossed aside and a cull of the Indigenous people living here occurred to make room for the newcomers. The total number slaughtered is unknown and widely disputed; however, scholars agree that the number living in both the US and Canada was somewhere between 10 and 18 million. An estimated 90 percent died after the arrival of Europeans from disease and conflict.

For those Indigenous that did survive, the system of working equally together for the betterment of the entire community, or egalitarianism, was in direct opposition to the European capitalism system. There was no way that these two systems could exist side by side. By this time, the number of European settlers was beginning to outweigh the number of Indigenous people. So it was inevitable that their system of government, laws and culture would become dominant. The land that was promised to the European settlers still legally belonged to the Indigenous, according to British Royal Proclamation of 1763; however, it was taken and given to the settlers anyway. The

Indigenous people were forced to move to less arable land far away from the newcomers. The British set up an Indian Affairs department that was mandated to ensure compliance to the new order of things. Their main goal was to do away with all the tribal systems and assimilate the Indigenous people into European systems by any means necessary so there would be no-one left to argue the legality of those treaties and no further obligation on the part of the Crown. As for the Indigenous women, their value in this new society was undermined completely and utterly. The men were used to continue to help fight any conflicts that arose; however, the forced imposition of the new patriarchal system disassociated Indigenous women from their traditional roles and diminished their power, status and freedom in all ways.

Invisible Victims

Katherine McCarthy

The Indian Act

After the War of 1812 that found Indigenous people fighting alongside the British against the United States, relations between Indigenous people and pre-Confederation Canada was at a fork in the road. Canada had to decide whether to 'abandon' the Indigenous people living there and abolish the Department of Indian Affairs, or to continue the Department but redefine its goals. The Indigenous people were strong military allies in war; however, a new era of peace saw Canada not needing those particular military alliances like before. Besides, more and more British settlers were moving to Canada, so if military was needed, they would do. And the British countrymen were less hassle. While some argued that it was philanthropy, obligation or simply 'the right thing to do', the reason they chose to take the Indigenous people under their wing, 'redeem them from savagery' and 'civilize them' probably had more to do with the economic ramifications of breaking the treaties that were signed and still binding in court today. Regardless, the decision made at that point in time severely impacted generations of Indigenous people in Canada and is the reason for the state of affairs today.

With the decision to 'adopt' the Indigenous as their own made, Canada was faced with the challenge of how to manage a great many different existing Indigenous nations. There was no way Canada was going to entertain the idea of dealing with each tribe on a nation-to-nation basis. So, following the mentality of thousands of years of capitalistic conquerors, the Indigenous people of Canada were going to have to assimilate and become just like the new white European settlers. In the meantime, they became 'wards of the state' until they were 'civilized.' From that time on, Canada had only one goal in mind for the Indigenous people: "Get rid of the Indian problem." Every policy enacted and every decision made since then has been done with that goal in mind.

The Indian Act is the insidious legislation that was created to govern and control every aspect of the lives of Indigenous people in Canada. Combining all other piece-meal legislation in place prior to that date, the new Indian Act was a coordinated tool by which a democratic society could legally subdue, manipulate and marginalize an entire race. Officially enacted in 1876, the policies under that Act were horrifying when they were birthed and, in some ways, they still are since much of it is still in place today. Paternalistic in nature and invasive in its administration, this Act allowed, and still allows, the Canadian government to oversee and alter the day-to-day living of registered Indigenous peoples and reserve communities. Most people are aware of the appalling apartheid system in South Africa that was established against the Indigenous people there and the atrocities they faced as a result of that system. What's not so commonly known is that South Africa's apartheid system was modeled after Canada's Indian Act.[26] Canada's model of Indian reserves, residential schools, segregation, and many other deeply racist systems actually inspired South Africa's oppressive regime. Author Linda Freeman offered in her book *The Ambiguous Champion* that officials from South Africa regularly came to Canada to see firsthand the system's success with keeping the Indigenous people in line.

For the Indigenous people living in Canada, The Indian Act ushered in a new era of forced assimilation towards European ways of life. In order for true assimilation to occur, the government knew separating people from their cultural stronghold and eliminating their governmental systems was the best way to start. Cultural ceremonies such as potlatches were among the first to be targeted. Potlatch ceremonies especially were the cornerstone to many Indigenous communities. It was there that new Chiefs were chosen (governance), wealth distributed among tribes (self sustainment), and celebrations of marriages and births took place (culture). Viewed as a deterrent to planned assimilation tactics, a complete ban on potlatches and other special ceremonies such as sun dances came into effect in 1880. Participating in any of these cultural ceremonies was from then on a criminal offense. Abolishing these events would be the same as a group of oppressors coming into Canada today and telling Christians that from now on it's illegal to be married in a church, or the equivalent to them saying our Canadian parliament could no longer meet and discuss policies without facing criminal charges. This ban on cultural ceremonies was in place for almost 75 years. It was only removed in 1951 once the general public, made aware of basic human rights after the atrocities of WWII, started to take notice of the poor treatment of Canada's Indigenous peoples. This was especially true once they discovered how many Indigenous people gave up their status in order to go fight for Canada in the brutal world war. But by then an entire generation was deprived of the cultural knowledge, teachings, and sacred ceremonies of Indigenous people, and an entire generation of self-governance knowledge was lost.

As a replacement system more in line with European system of government, the Department of Indian Affairs imposed the mandatory 'band council system' which is still in place today. Under this system, a Chief and council was elected by the people; however, they were accountable to the Department of Indian Affairs (i.e., Canadian government). Elections were every three years at first, then later every two years; only males over the age of 23 were allowed to vote; and the chiefs had very little in the way of power. Anything to do with land or finances was managed by the Department. This type of system severely impacted all Indigenous nations. It was unfamiliar, nonsensical and eradicated any leadership authority within a tribe. The ridiculously brief term of a Chief and council's time in office alone led to great political instability and left little hope to develop any type of long-term economic initiatives for the communities or to build anything resembling a solid foundation. But I'm sure the Canadian government knew that.

In 1879, Canada started looking at instituting residential schools based on the American model. It was felt that separating the Indigenous children from their families entirely was the best way to break the link to their culture and identity. Canada's first Prime Minister, Sir John A. MacDonald, was enthusiastically in favor of this plan. By 1930, there were 80 residential schools operating across Canada. The federal government estimated that 150,000 Indigenous children passed through the system.[27] The last one didn't close its doors until 1996.

In 1885, the Canadian government instituted the pass system under The Indian Act. They said it was to keep the European settlers safe from any "rebel Indians", but more likely it was another means of control. If an Indigenous person wanted to leave the reserve they were forced to live on, they needed permission from the reserve's Indian Agent. Conversely, no outsider was permitted to visit or do business on a reserve without permission. This was a way to control trade or sale of goods without the government's knowledge. Indigenous farmers needed a pass to go off the reserve to sell their crops. If the Agent was away when they went to get a pass, after sometimes having to travel days to get to the Agent's place, their crops were left to spoil. A parent wanting to visit their child at a residential school was also required to have a pass. And agents were encouraged to issue passes for this reason no more than four times a year, if at all.[28] The pass system was in place until 1951 as well.

In the late 1800s, some of the Indigenous reserves in Saskatchewan were doing so well growing and selling their crops, they were perceived as a threat to the European settlers. An amendment to the Indian Act fixed this by adding a "Permit System" to the legislation. Basically Indigenous people were now restricted in how much they could sell. They needed a permit in order to sell. They also needed a permit to buy. And that included the clothes they wore. Under this system, the settlers were also restricted in buying goods from Indigenous people.[29] Control all around.

If an Indigenous person wanted to go to university, join the military, or become a member of the clergy, they had to give up their status entirely. Until 1960, if an Indigenous person wanted to vote in a Canadian election, they had to give up their status. Appearing in pool halls or gambling was not permitted. Buying ammunition or alcohol was not permitted. The Act forbade Indigenous people from speaking their language and from practicing their traditional religion. Appearing in ceremonial dress without the permission of the Indian Agent was not allowed either.

In 1920, testimony from the Deputy Superintendent of Indian Affairs, Duncan

Invisible Victims

Campbell Scott, to the House of Commons had him publicly referring to 'The Indian Problem'.

"I want to get rid of the Indian problem. I do not think as a matter of fact, that the country ought to continuously protect a class of people who are able to stand alone ... Our objective is to continue until there is not a single Indian in Canada that has not been absorbed into the body politic and there is no Indian question, and no Indian Department, that is the whole object of this Bill."[30]

Indigenous people started to fight back around this time by organizing political groups to insist the government of Canada honor the treaties previously signed between nations, especially with respect to land rights. The Indian Act stepped in once again and outlawed the hiring of lawyers and legal counsel, barring Indigenous people from fighting for what was theirs. Most of these political groups disbanded as a result.

Indigenous women were even more oppressed by the very sexist Indian Act. Not a huge surprise there since the Act was legislated by a patriarchal system, and non-Indigenous women suffered oppression under those systems for centuries. To go from their former way of life with position and respect to one where gender bias was the norm was extremely difficult and challenging for Indigenous women. According to the Indian Act, Indigenous women were not allowed to vote in band councils until the privilege was granted in 1951. They went from positions of power to being unable to vote in elections, from managing the resources of communities to having no say in the governance of their communities. The roles of men and women were always complementary and equal. However, under this new Indian Act, women weren't even considered people. So for 116 years, Indigenous women were discriminated against. And it was completely legal to do so.

The Act had some very discriminatory marriage provisions as well. If an Indigenous woman married a non-Indigenous man, they lost status for themselves and any children she had. It was not this way with Indigenous men, though. They could marry a non-Indigenous woman, maintain their status, their children's status, and gain status for their non-Indigenous wife.

"Legislation stated that a status Indian woman who married a non-Indian man would cease to be an Indian. She would lose her status, and with it, she would lose treaty benefits, health benefits, the right to live on her reserve, the right to inherit her family property, and even the right to be buried on

the reserve with her ancestors. However, if an Indian man married a non-status woman, he would keep all his rights. Even if an Indian woman married another Indian man, she would cease to be a member of her own band, and become a member of his. If a woman was widowed, or abandoned by her husband, she would become enfranchised and lose status altogether...In all the situations, a woman's status was entirely dependent on their (sic) husband."[31]

So if a woman was abandoned by her husband, she could not return to her community. Where did she go? What options were available to her? The freedom for an Indigenous woman to marry whom she wanted was not granted until 1985. If a woman's husband decided to enfranchise his status (i.e. sell it back to the government), it would automatically mean the woman's and her children's status would be lost as well. All of this made the Indigenous woman completely dependent on men. Another quite unbelievable part of the Indian Act was the stipulation that women were expected to uphold a "good, moral character" as determined by the Indian Agent. So the non-Indigenous representative basically acted as a sexual policing agent for the government who had the power to jail a woman he felt was unchaste. No room for abuse there.

Katherine McCarthy

Residential Schools

Canada's Church-run, government-funded residential school system was created for the purpose of separating Indigenous children from their parents, communities, and culture, and to aggressively assimilate them into the dominant European society. For well over a century, children as young as 7 and until they reached the age of 16, attended these schools. Attendance was compulsory, and agents were employed by the government to ensure the children attended. Children were often forcibly removed from their communities and their families threatened with fines or jail time if they failed to send their children. Many children didn't have any contact with their families for 10 months at a time and, in some cases, years.

The first school was established in the 1840s and the last one in Saskatchewan didn't close its doors until 1996. At the peak of the program in the 1930s, there were 80 residential schools in operation. Over the entire time period in which they existed, the schools numbered over 130.

Invisible Victims

It is estimated that 150,000 children went through the system. Of this number, 80,000 of these survivors are still alive today. The Truth and Reconciliation Commission of Canada, a group that led the investigation into residential schools, confirmed 3,200 child deaths. However, because of poor record keeping and destroyed files, the exact number will never be known. A reasonable estimate puts that number closer to 6,000. The children died from disease and malnutrition at these schools. Some residential schools had a 60 percent mortality rate. Some students were subjected to science experiments. Children were subjected to abuse at the hands of the staff and administrators, often physically, always emotionally, and sometimes sexually. The experiences of the Indigenous people at these schools were hidden for many decades, until Indigenous people found the strength, courage and support to bring them to light.

Stories of the student's time at these schools are heartrending. Ripped from their loving families at age 7 and taken to an industrial-sized institution, the first order of business was to separate them from any siblings or friends, strip the children of their clothes and belongings, literally, and de-louse them whether they needed it or not. They then had their hair cut off, which in Indigenous culture was especially traumatic as long hair holds special significance. They were given uniforms, and their native clothing and moccasins were thrown in the garbage. That was just Day 1.

For the children, life at these schools was unfamiliar, lonely and often terrifying. They were not permitted to speak their language. They had to learn English or French only. So until they learned it, they could not communicate with anyone. The documentary, *We Were Children*,[32] recounts the story of two survivors and how the children were made to hold onto their tongues for hours, with drool slipping down their little faces, if they were caught speaking their native language. The schools were usually underfunded. Therefore, many children were forced into labor to maintain the facilities. The full extent of the abuse suffered by the children is only now coming to light. What is known is that throughout the years, all students lived in substandard conditions, suffered many types of abuses, and were completely disassociated from their families and culture, thereby experiencing cultural genocide. The exact amount of sexual and physical abuse is hard to determine; however, there were 37,951 claims submitted by survivors for injuries resulting from physical and sexual abuse[33] at residential schools. So that provided some indication.

    Despite the fact that this dark chapter in Canada's history is now exposed, it does not bring the legacy of residential schools to an end. The impacts of forced disassociation from culture, disruption of families and communities, humiliation and improper health and living conditions at these schools has been the cause of inter-generational trauma and won't be fixed with a settlement or an apology. Children who were abused went on to abuse others. Many developed addictions as a means of coping. Many who were treated like prisoners in the schools ended up in prisons in their adult life. The children of survivors, their partners, their grandchildren, extended families and communities were and are all impacted. It will take many years to properly heal from the legacy of residential schools.

Katherine McCarthy

The Sixties Scoop

The Sixties Scoop was another assimilation policy established by the Canadian government in the 1960s when some residential schools were starting to shut down. Poor quality as they were, there was still a cost involved in running them. A new cheaper assimilation policy was needed. Adoption was becoming more commonplace around this time and, from the government's perspective, they would save a whole lot of money if non-Indigenous people adopted Indigenous children and did for them what they had been trying to do for over a century..."to kill the Indian in the child." Under the guise of a national child welfare program, the Sixties Scoop was born. Indigenous children were apprehended by child welfare agencies and adopted out to non-Indigenous homes -- sometimes without consent or knowledge of the parents. Thousands of Indigenous children were removed from their families and placed in homes in Canada, the United States and overseas. The program actually lasted for decades and stretched well past the '60s into the mid-1980s.

Raven Sinclair, associate professor of social work at the University of Regina in Saskatoon, and herself a Sixties Scoop adoptee, stated that "between the 1950s and the end of the 1960s, the percentage of children in care who were aboriginal skyrocketed from less than one percent to roughly 40 percent." The exact number of Sixties Scoop adoptees is unknown; however, "between the 1960s and 1985, the federal government estimates that just over 11,000 children were removed from their families and adopted out. But the real number may be anywhere from 20,000 and 50,000 children, according to Sinclair. "Child welfare practices sometimes labeled children as non-status or Métis," said Sinclair. "And we believe that was in order to make them seem more adoptable."[34]

A lot of the adoptive parents weren't aware the child they took in was stolen. One Sixties Scoop adoptee, Nina Segalowitz, says she was stolen when her birth parents brought her into the hospital for treatment as an infant and they had issues filling out the paperwork. They were told to leave the infant in their care and to come back the next day when they would have the right medication. When they came back the next day, their baby girl was gone. Social workers working in child welfare didn't have any special training in Indigenous culture. They based their assessments on whether a child was being cared for or not on what they knew from their own experience, which was normally a very different non-Indigenous Canadian society. Often mistakes were made and children were assessed in need of care unnecessarily. "For example, when social workers entered the homes of families subsisting on a traditional Aboriginal diet of dried game, fish, and berries, and didn't see fridges or cupboards stocked in typical Euro-Canadian fashion, they assumed that the adults in the home were not providing for their children. Additionally, upon seeing the social problems reserve communities faced, such as poverty, unemployment, and addiction, some social workers felt a duty to protect the local children. In many cases, Aboriginal parents who were living in poverty but otherwise providing caring homes had their children taken from them with little or no warning and absolutely no consent."[35]

Adopted children growing up with suppressed identities often experience problems later in life. Some of these children were told they were French or Italian. Their records could not be opened unless both the child and the parents agreed. The laws around child apprehension weren't changed until 1985. However, damage was already done to at least 11,000 more Indigenous children in Canada.

Katherine McCarthy

Forced Sterilizations & Eugenics

Eugenics. A very scary and inherently racist word indeed. Sir Francis Gaulton, a British sociologist, invented the term "eugenics"[36] in 1883, building it from its Latin roots meaning "good in birth" or "noble in heredity." The science of eugenics, which came into prominence during the late nineteenth century, was all about improving the human race. Eugenicists believed that natural selection (more commonly known as Charles Darwin's 'survival of the fittest') was insufficient, and they sought to influence human evolution by weeding out "undesirables." A combination of heavy immigration and a fear that undesirables were reproducing at a high rate contributed to the popularization of eugenics in Canada. Such well-known figures as Emily Murphy and J.S. Woodsworth were avowed eugenicists.[37] In the context of colonization, discussions around population control of the Indigenous peoples often included eugenics. "By the 1930s, some academics, doctors, psychiatrists and politicians viewed the sterilization of 'undesirables' as a solution to crime, poverty, and the growing costs of institutionalization. A wide variety of marginalized groups were targeted, including the poor, Aboriginal peoples, Métis, new immigrants, and 'the feeble-minded', those with perceived intellectual disabilities or mental illnesses. More women than men experienced forced sterilization."[38]

Alberta was the first province to enact legislation, the Sexual Sterilization Act, and from this a Eugenics Board was created that recommended sterilization as a condition of release from mental institutions. Nine years later, the Act was amended to allow sterilizations without consent from those deemed "mentally defective." Between 1928 and 1972, Alberta's Eugenics Board approved 99 percent of its 4,785 cases.[39] The province of British Columbia also enacted sexual sterilization legislation in 1933; however, it maintained the necessity of consent to perform the procedure. Therefore, the number of people sterilized in that province was much less than Alberta at a few hundred cases. Other provinces may not have had actual legislation in place; however, forced or coercive sterilizations did occur regardless.

So how does this relate to Indigenous women specifically? If we look at the numbers from Alberta, of those sterilized from 1928 and 1972, 6 to 8 percent were Indigenous, even though Indigenous peoples only made up 3 percent of the population at the time. So a disproportionate number of Indigenous people were being sterilized whether they wanted to be or not. A closer look at the time period between 1969 and 1972 indicated a staggering 25 percent[40] of those being sterilized were Indigenous. Recall what was stated earlier that, around that time, residential schools were starting to close or wind down. The government needed more affordable ways to control the population of Indigenous people. Dr. Karen Stote, professor at Sir Wilfred Laurier University, authored a book about the sterilization of Indigenous women as an act of genocide. She argued that forced sterilization was an act of genocide and that the reason was to reduce those whom the government is obligated to: *"...the consistent undermining of Aboriginal women and their reproductive lives through policies and practices like coercive sterilization has been part of a longstanding attack against Indigenous ways of life in an effort to reduce those to whom the federal government has obligations, and in order to gain access to lands and resources. Coercive sterilization should not be viewed in isolation from the larger context in which it has taken place, just as other policies such as residential schools cannot be separated from the larger purposes they have served."*[41] So in addition to the residential schools, the Sixties Scoop and all the other oppressive tactics Canada had in play, the utilization of existing eugenics legislation made sense for them. All they needed to do was have the Eugenic board, which was made up of judges, psychiatrists and social workers, agree that their targeted patients were mentally ill. Many doctors were in favor of these eugenics policies, and since psychiatry and social work were still relatively new fields of science that were struggling for acceptance among the medical community, they were more than willing to agree. The psychological community carved a niche out for itself by creating the intelligence tests to be used by the Eugenics Board in determining whether or not someone should have sterilization forced on them.

Many problems existed with this new policy. The IQ tests used to determine mental deficiency were written in English and based on specific Western European knowledge. Since they were not designed with the various Indigenous populations in mind, the Indigenous people often scored poorly on them. If you scored within the criteria as having a mental deficiency, you had no choice but to undergo sterilization. There were problems with the consent forms as well. In the case of youth where consent was required, there were instances where a consent form was mailed out stating, "unless we hear anything back from you in the next two weeks, sterilization will go forth on your child." Parents or guardians who moved around looking for work or who were unlucky to not receive the letter in time were devastated to find out they were too late. If the parent didn't respond for whatever reason, all that was needed was the signature of the Minister of Health. In 1955, some provincial institutions adopted a generic form for patients to sign that gave the hospital permission to perform a sterilization in the future if need be, thereby canceling out the need for consent.[42]

    The legislation may no longer be in place, however, Indigenous women are still being badgered in hospitals about being sterilized. Just last year, Saskatoon Health was made to issue a formal apology to two Indigenous women for their medical staff pressuring the women into having tubal ligation surgeries. One consented after being told the procedure was reversible and she was so tired after just having a baby that she just wanted them to go away and leave her alone. On the operating table and under medication, she was objecting and telling the surgeon she didn't want to do it. They did it anyway. The other woman being badgered by a nurse and a social worker after having a baby was saved when the obstetrician came in the room and called them off.[43]

Katherine McCarthy

Role of DNA

One last thing to discuss about the root causes of violence towards Indigenous women is the role that DNA plays. This is really important to healing the inter-generational effects of all the government's assimilation policies and programs from the past. Scientists have found that memories can be passed down through the generations by our DNA. Tests performed on mice showed that they "can pass on learned information about traumatic or stressful experiences – in this case a fear of the smell of cherry blossom – to subsequent generations."[44]

Our bodies are designed to handle stress. However, if that stress is chronic and prolonged, the body remembers by transferring that knowledge from the brain to what's called an epigenome. Besides mice, scientists have been doing tests on the children and grandchildren of Holocaust survivors. While this field of study is still very new, *"according to the new insights of behavioral epigenetics, traumatic experiences in our past, or in our recent ancestors' past, leave molecular scars adhering to our DNA. Jews whose great-grandparents were chased from their Russian shtetls; Chinese whose grandparents lived through the ravages of the Cultural Revolution; young immigrants from Africa whose parents survived massacres; adults of every ethnicity who grew up with alcoholic or abusive parents -- all carry with them more than just memories."*[45] Or residential school students who survived the abuse meted out to them for years. It's possible that the scars of those traumatic memories imposed by all of the government's racist policies have been attached to the DNA of Canada's Indigenous peoples. If the scientists are correct, it will take generations to undo the damage. However, the scientists are confident it can be reversed. They say that if your grandmother received loving care and nurturing, those positive experiences will attach themselves to the epigenome as well. And they will be passed on as well as any strengths.

Katherine McCarthy

MMIW Crimes

Carol Nora King (SK)

Invisible Victims

In 2008, Carol Nora King, a Mi'kmaq woman originally from a small rural community on the west coast of Newfoundland, Mattis Point, had moved "out west" to another small community in the province of Saskatchewan to work. She purchased a farmhouse after securing a job in the construction industry in Herschel, Saskatchewan, about 150 kilometers outside the larger city of Saskatoon. Though far from her home, Carol remained very close with her family back in Newfoundland and was never entirely happy living so far away from them. She spoke on the phone or chatted online every day without fail to either of her three sisters, brother or her parents on the east coast of the country. After three years living there, Carol, then 40 years old, decided the distance was too much and she wanted to move back home. She put her house on the market to sell with plans to move back to be with her family.

On the afternoon of August 6, 2011, Carol was chatting online via webcam with her sister Brenda, as well as her parents, Carl and Yvonne King. She mentioned having an appointment that evening with the Rosetown RCMP to report some disturbing happenings that occurred the night before and to file a harassment complaint. Unfortunately, Carol did not make it to that appointment. She was supposed to call her family back that night to let them know how it went, but when no-one heard from her and every effort to reach her failed, the family immediately called the police. They wanted to file an official report so the police could go into her house to see if anything was amiss. However, the police argued Carol had probably just taken off and would eventually show up. Despite the insistence from her family that that would not be in her character, for three days they refused to take any action. They pleaded with the RCMP to go look at the house. They explained Carol's personal situation and that she was being harassed by her ex-boyfriend and she was very afraid of him. They were very concerned for her welfare.

Still the police did nothing. They refused to go into her house to see if anything was amiss, even with the family's permission, and they wouldn't file an official missing person report. That is, until some family members booked flights across the country to physically look for their loved one, while others started talking to the media and started a social media campaign on Facebook to find out where she was. Once her family showed up in Herschel, things moved rather quickly. An official missing persons report was filed on August 9th, her case was given "top priority" and a search

Invisible Victims

and rescue team was engaged to look for her missing car. Witnesses were questioned and all leads were being chased down. Given the small population of the community, however, there were only three neighbors that could have seen anything. One was away due to a death in their family, one didn't see anything, and the other was her ex-boyfriend who stated he was out of town working the past few weeks.

When police finally spoke to the media, RCMP spokesman Cpl. Rob King confirmed that the missing woman had an appointment "to give more information and a statement **on an ongoing investigation that she was involved with."** She never showed up.[46] It was never officially revealed by police whether the ongoing investigation they were referring to was the harassment or something else.

The next day on August 10, after an aerial search for her car, Carol's vehicle, a grey PT Cruiser, was found submerged in a watery slough in an abandoned yard near Herschel. A slough is a deep hole in a road that is usually filled with water and mud. They can be quite large and some are large enough to easily hide a vehicle. Strangely, it was located in the opposite direction of where her appointment was. The vehicle was removed and sent to the lab for forensic examination. Unfortunately, there was no sign of Carol.

Katherine McCarthy

In the days that followed, the family, worried beyond comprehension, offered a reward of $25,000 for information leading to the safe return of Carol. Ground searches continued by law enforcement including the use of cadaver-sniffing dogs borrowed from the Calgary RCMP around her property and the area where her abandoned car was found. Many volunteers assisted with the search. Her sister Brenda remained in the area searching abandoned places, making public pleas to anyone who had information to come forward, handing out missing person flyers while remaining hopeful and praying that Carol was alive and would be found safe. Candlelight vigils were held back in her hometown in Newfoundland for her safe return. The police, who did now seem to be doing everything they could, found no clues but did declare her disappearance was suspicious.

Sadly, on August 27, roughly three weeks after Carol had been reported missing, a body was found five miles from her house. Herschel-born resident and volunteer searcher Kevin Booth heard the public request from the RCMP for local residents to look around all rural properties and felt compelled to drive from Saskatoon where he was living to help search the area where he grew up. "Once I had heard that the dogs from Calgary had no luck, seeing as how I knew the area so well, I just felt it was something I had to do," said Booth.[47] He drove to Herschel that morning with his all-terrain vehicle in his truck and asked the owner of the property, Greg Martin, if he could look around since he was familiar with the area. An hour later, he made the discovery. He drove to the RCMP detachment and led them back to the scene.

While the family hoped and prayed this was not their beloved Carol, the remains were sent to Saskatoon for identification. Forensic anthropologist Ernie Walker confirmed shortly after, through the use of dental records, that the remains were in fact Carol King.

Hundreds of people expressed their remorse at the loss of Carol in a Facebook Group called "In Loving Memory of Carol King" and online. Hundreds more paid their respects in person at the funeral held in her hometown in Newfoundland. Initial thoughts were that Carol had accidentally driven her car into the slough and was injured but managed to get out. Perhaps she tried to walk for help but later succumbed to her injuries. That theory was overturned once the police declared her death to be suspicious. Strangely, though, they would not disclose either her cause of death or details about the condition of her remains.

Katherine McCarthy

While family and friends mourned, the police continued their investigation. Mid-September 2011 brought a public request from the RCMP for residents of Herschel and nearby Rosetown to keep their eyes open for any personal items that may have belonged to Carol, specifically her purse that had never been found. Obviously they felt her purse might hold some answers as to what happened to her. Despite the public pleas for any information that could help solve the crime and the reward for information being offered, no leads were forthcoming and no arrests were made.

Rumors in the town about who was responsible for Carol's death were rife. Strange thing was that the exact spot where Carol's body was found was the most isolated spot in the entire area. Overgrown with tall grass and weeds, just off a seldom-used road, it was a perfect spot to dispose of something not wanting to be found. It was believed that only someone with knowledge of the area would know how ideal that spot would be to cover any tracks. Stranger still was the fact that that exact spot where she was found was already searched once before – by Carol's own sister Brenda.[48] Obviously Carol's remains were moved there later. The town talk was that Carol had confided in friends about her fear of her ex-boyfriend, David Caissie, and his recent erratic

Invisible Victims

behavior. She believed her ex was spying on her and prowling around her property late at night. Carol reported this to the local police and expressed her fear of him. They questioned Caissie's whereabouts at the time of her disappearance and he had a solid alibi. He was allegedly working in another province, Alberta, that was verified by two other men who worked for Caissie. This didn't help with the rumors, though, as Caissie had a sordid history of violence. In 1998, he was convicted of a violent sexual assault against a woman. He forced a woman at knife-point into her vehicle, drove to a remote location and raped her on the hood of her vehicle. He was sentenced to serve five years in prison for the attack.

    The case of Carol's 'suspicious death' took an eerie turn when in early December, Greg Martin, owner of the abandoned property where Carol's body was found, discovered a granite stone memorial bearing a cross erected in the spot where her car was found. On it a passage was etched: "Please don't give him your HATE, he's not WORTH it. The Lord he cam (sic) and got me, and took me far away. Remember, I wasn't in my body when the DEVIL came to play. WHY?"[49] It was reported that part of this passage was taken from a poem written by the daughter of Cindy Ramos who was murdered in California in 2009.[50] August

6, 2009, to be precise. Carol disappeared that same day exactly two years later.

The owner of the property said he had no idea who erected the memorial without his permission but he was also sent a signed letter with an obituary. The contents, however, were not made public and the signature was illegible. The local newspaper, *Rosetown Eagle*, also received a letter but decided not to publish it due to its deranged nature. It was handed over to police who decided to keep it quiet for three weeks. The whole suspicious memorial and the strange notes did not become known to the public until interest in the case flared up again three weeks later when local fire crews were called to Carol's house on Sunday, December 18 at 9:30am. The blaze and smoke of the fire in her house had, by the time the fire crew got there, caused significant damage. It didn't take long to make a determination that arson was the cause.

Suspicion that David Caissie had murdered Carol made life unbearable for the ex-boyfriend in small town Herschel. He decided to break his silence and speak to the media for the first time on December 21. In an interview with CBC News, Caissie says, "I want them to find out who did this...so that people will know that I had nothing to do with it."[51] He says he would never have harmed the woman

Invisible Victims

he loved. He also denied setting the fire, claiming to have no knowledge of it until he saw it on TV. Caissie admitted to having a financial stake in the house, so why would he want to destroy it. Apparently when he discovered Carol had put the house on the market with plans to move back to Newfoundland with her family, he put a lien on the house in order to ensure he would get his fair share of the proceeds he felt he was entitled to after a four-year relationship with her. Despite his public plea of innocence in any wrongdoing, family members and public opinion were not swayed to his side. Carol's family knew that Caissie had been harassing her for weeks before her disappearance and that she was afraid of him. Caissie insisted this was not true and that even though Carol was aware of his violent past, she trusted him enough to stay with him for four years. And then there is the matter of his airtight alibi. At the time when Carol disappeared, Caissie was in another province working and two other people that worked for him could verify this to be true.

Further mystery was added when it became known to police that this most recent fire was not the first time a residence of Carol's burned. The first one was in September 2009 when a second home on the property burned to the ground. The second was in July 2010 when her fifth wheel trailer went missing and was found burned a few weeks later. Strangely, it was found in the same slough where her car was found. Police admitted to finding the string of fires interesting and would be taking a closer look at the first two. [52]

An anniversary of crimes is usually when emotions and discussions resurface, details are talked about again and new tips pour in for the police to investigate. The first anniversary of Carol's disappearance brought a statement from police that the case is still active, an ongoing investigation, and that it's still one of the top priorities of their major crime unit. Between 40 and 60 investigators work this unit; however, they did not reveal what specifically they have been investigating.[53] The third anniversary of her death brought a single news article from Global News rehashing a few details of the crime, a brief mention of how the family was raw with emotion when contacted, and a focus on how the community of Herschel is starting to feel safe again now that "the spotlight is slowly fading." A new and different lead investigator stated that he couldn't comment on where they were today compared to three years ago but that the case was still a priority and they are following up on leads as they come in. [54] The fourth anniversary brought another rehashing of the events, albeit brief, and another new and different investigator. This time, however, comments from Carol's sister Brenda showed a sadness for their loss, yet discontent toward the lack of progress on solving Carol's case. "Everything is pretty much the same. You never hear anything from them," Brenda said of the Royal Canadian Mounted Police in Saskatchewan. But that doesn't stop her from calling. "They're saying it's not a cold case, but we never hear any information."[55] Interestingly enough, a different news source stated that their information came from the historical case division. "Mounties said they are no closer to solving the homicide. The historical case division says there are no new developments as they continue to follow up on tips and stay in regular contact with King's family."[56]

So where does the murder case of Carol King stand today? Almost five years later, the case seems to be very much in stasis mode. While the police say it's still an active investigation, there is nothing new and no charges have been laid. The family has still not been given an official cause of death even. How could this case have possibly gone cold? Multiple crime scenes, purposeful torching of her house, a mysterious memorial and notes sent to various people in the town, her car –

the town of Herschel should be crawling with physical evidence. Not to mention the obvious motives of people close to her (potential criminal charges for stalking, financial motives, the ongoing investigation the police alluded to in the very early days, etc.) And an even more important question to ask is why did the police not take her stalking allegations seriously nor her subsequent mysterious disappearance when her family insisted something was wrong? To make matters worse for both the family and for those keeping tabs on the number of missing and murdered Indigenous women in Canada, the police never did and still refuse to officially rule Carol's death a homicide. Rather, they continue to keep her case out of the official police statistical counts for MMIW by deeming it a "suspicious death".

Invisible Victims

Katherine McCarthy

Toronto's Sisters of Spirit

In 2013, three young First Nation women living in Toronto, Ontario met sudden deaths within three months of each other. Cheyenne Fox (20), Terra-Janine Gardner (26) and Bella Laboucan-McLean (25) all died under horrible and mysterious circumstances. Two of these deaths were quickly deemed suicides by investigators – within hours actually -- while the third death was ruled "suspicious." Despite this emerging pattern of mysterious deaths among First Nation young women, police did not put out any kind of public advisory. Nor was there much media coverage to speak of. Shamefully, most of us haven't even heard their names.

On April 24, 2013, 20-year-old Cheyenne Santana Marie Fox, a member of Sheguiandah First Nation[57] in the province of Ontario, fell 24 stories from a downtown Toronto condo to her death. Cheyenne's father was notified by police early the next morning that she had fallen from a balcony at 10:30 the evening before. By 8 am that morning, within mere hours, it was ruled a suicide. The only witness – her client who was with her at the time. Cheyenne was a sex worker.

Cheyenne grew up in Sioux Lookout, northwest of Thunder Bay, Ontario, splitting her time between living with her father or her mother. Free spirited and feisty, Cheyenne wasn't scared of much. Her father described her as "very compassionate, very caring and she didn't judge anybody."[58] Her cultural roots were very strong. She often attended drumming socials, powwows and smudging ceremonies. She was a jingle dress dancer. A jingle dress is a traditional native dress adorned with little tin cones that tinkle with every movement. A jingle dress dancer is a very important role in an Indigenous community. They are considered spiritual healers – not a role that Cheyenne would have taken lightly. And not one that those with suicidal thoughts would be drawn to. So strong was her fighting spirit, she often attended Indigenous activist movements such as Idle No More rallies with her politically active father.

Like most of us, Cheyenne also had a darker side. Her family admitted she was troubled, but not troubled enough to commit suicide. Her adolescent years were tumultuous. She had issues with authority, was often angry, distant, and began drinking at an early age. At 15 years old, she was pregnant and had a beautiful baby boy, Xavier. After a couple years of living on Manitoulin Island with Xavier and his father, a still very young Cheyenne was just too restless. She left Xavier in the care of his father and moved to Toronto. The big city was not all she expected, though. She had hoped to get an apartment and work towards becoming a beautician. Instead she ended up in a women's shelter and eventually was lured into the sex trade. In 2012, she was sexually assaulted, and it's reported this assault is still in the court system to be tried. She spent a brief time in jail for fighting and, when she got out, she began working as an escort. A few weeks later, Cheyenne was dead.

The night of her fall is shrouded in mystery. What does the family know about Cheyenne's last night? The police report states that the condo owner was male and that the client had requested she come there for sexual services. They know that the condo owner told police that shortly after she arrived, she wanted to leave but he blocked the door. The police say the 'john' also tried to stop her from jumping over the balcony.[59] Police refuse to release his name or address or tell the family where it was that Cheyenne actually died. Some accounts say that she had been drinking heavily earlier that evening. Several 911 calls relating back to Cheyenne were made that night. The first was made around 6 pm from someone who witnessed Cheyenne jump from a slow-moving taxicab on Highway 401. The caller was reportedly the one who picked her up and then dropped her off at a condo on Harrison Garden Blvd. It is alleged she jumped from the vehicle because the cab driver was sexually assaulting her.[60] Another call was made from the condo she was in around 8 pm. This one was from the owner of the condo stating that Cheyenne was there, intoxicated, and would not leave. Still another source alleges two other 911 calls were made that night from third parties. One was concerning a woman briefly dangling from a balcony in that area. It is unconfirmed whether this was actually Cheyenne or not. Then a third 911 call was made just moments before she supposedly 'jumped' off the balcony. Again the call was made by the condo owner/'john' who insists she jumped from the balcony. He is the only witness.

Cheyenne's father, John Fox, demanded then that police treat her death as a homicide. He and all his family strongly believed, and still do believe, Cheyenne would not have committed suicide. He has filed a lawsuit against the Toronto Police, the police services board and the Canadian government alleging they failed to protect Cheyenne the night she died. After all the 911 calls about her, they refused to take any action to protect her welfare. He has publicly stated that Cheyenne had committed to going to rehab at the end of April and had arranged her place for that to happen. He strongly asserts that while troubled, she was not suicidal. "We need justice for these girls," Fox says. "Every day, I live and breathe to get justice. There's nothing in the world that's going to stop me. Nothing at all." [61] Possibly even more important than justice is knowing the truth. Knowing exactly where Cheyenne died will allow the family to perform the proper spirit ceremony. The Fox family is very spiritual and culturally strong. In following with the Anishinabe traditions, they need to know where she died. Her spirit will not rest until this is done.

Not even a month later, on May 14, 26-year-old Terra-Janine Gardner was struck and killed by a freight train near Yonge St. and Summerhill Avenue, a popular spot for people to drink by the tracks, while in the company of two other people. Police ruled out foul play and again quickly deemed it an accident. Suspiciously, though, Terra was a star witness in a murder investigation and had already testified in the pre-trial a few weeks before. Her friends stated that she was receiving death threats about testifying further and was scared to do so.

Katherine McCarthy

APTN National News reported that Terra had been receiving death threats and was dubbed a rat for providing information about the beating death of First Nations man Leo Buswa, 42, in August 2010. Buswa was badly beaten and died a month later in the hospital. Blake Paul of Moose Factory, Ontario, was charged in the second degree murder and arrested in 2012 hiding in Eskanosi First

Invisible Victims

Nation in Nova Scotia. In April 2013, Terra reluctantly testified in the preliminary trial as a witness to the beating. She did not want to testify. She understood the rules of the streets and she was fearful of the consequences of testifying. According to Doug Johnson, street pastor at Sanctuary Ministries (an organization in Toronto that helps struggling people) in Toronto, she failed to show up to testify on two separate occasions because she didn't want to do it. However, the police tracked her down and threatened they would keep her held in custody if she didn't testify. She finally submitted. Also according to the Minister Johnson, *"They did not give her adequate protection for testifying...in a major murder trial where she is being called a rat and being threatened and we had to literally beg to get her a second night in a hotel and she was testifying for five straight days. They just wanted to give her the first night. She's homeless. She's vulnerable."* [62]

Turns out he was right. Terra returned to the same streets she called home. The same streets where she was receiving those threats, and sadly, a mere few weeks later, Terra met a very untimely and horrible death. Without their star witness, Blake Paul took a deal of two years in prison for the lesser charge of manslaughter[63] in the violent death of Buswa.

Katherine McCarthy

The Minister Johnson stated that Terra was thought of very highly at Sanctuary. Terra, meaning Earth, "...was a lovely women with a whip-smart sense of humor Someone who was very tough and able to handle herself on the street. But also subject to much violence and abuse herself." She volunteered and helped out at Sanctuary and attended many hours of counseling "She was growing," said Johnson. "She was changing. She was talking about things she could do differently in life when she was tragically struck by a train..."[64] A video interview of Terra[65] is still available on the amazing website "Invisible People" - a vlog (video blog) that brings awareness to the homeless, an attempt to make the 'invisible' visible. What struck me watching her speak is that her intelligence and compassion is obvious to everyone but her. Her answer to the interviewer's question "If you had three wishes, what would they be?" shows a heart-rending level of compassion and vulnerability. She wished for her to be able to change her life, her boyfriend to be able to change his life and for her family to love her more.

So what happened to Terra that she chose to live on the streets of Toronto? Why did having that cloak of invisibility mean so much to her? Her mother lived in Nigigoonsiminikaaning First Nation in northern Ontario and her father lived in Toronto. She spent time living with both parents; however, she could not seem to settle in either place. Her mom, Virginia, was a victim of the Sixties Scoop program previously discussed. Virginia ran away from her adopted home when she was 14 and suffered many issues herself as a result of the cultural genocide she endured. After things didn't work out with Terra's father, as a young resourceless female, Virginia lost custody of Terra and her brother Jay to her father, who gave them to their paternal grandparents to raise. When Terra and Jay were old enough to decide where they wanted to live, they both chose their mother. Terra stayed a couple of years, but Virginia lost custody once again to Family and Child Services when she was unable to maintain electricity in the house in which they lived. Terra went back to live with her father; however, she was conflicted and torn up about leaving her mother.

At 18, Terra had her first boyfriend and suffered two miscarriages. The loss sent her spinning out of control and she disappeared for about three weeks. She admitted to having suicidal thoughts at that time but would never do that to her brother. But she did start drinking, and excessively. Unwilling to move up north with her mother and unable to live with her father in Toronto, she lived in shelters for a while. But even the shelters weren't a safe haven for her. After being badly beaten at one shelter, she found solace sleeping as close as possible to the earth, like her name, on the grass in the parks. And that's where she liked to stay. Five months later, sweet Terra was dead.

On July 20, 2013, 25-year-old Bella Laboucan-McLean fell 31 stories from a downtown Toronto high-rise condo to her death. A recent graduate from the Fashion Arts Program at Humber College in Toronto, Bella attended an event earlier that evening and then an after party at the condo. Five other people besides Bella were in the small 800-sq.ft. condo that night, but no-one called the police after she fell. A neighbor who heard an altercation and then her fall notified police. For 12 hours police were going door to door trying to find out which condo she fell from in order to identify her. When the call finally came in 12 hours later, the police questioned the others who were at the party about what happened to Bella. No-one saw anything and no-one knew anything. Yet all of her belongings were still there in the condo...purse, wallet, shoes, phone...but no-one called the police to report her missing.

Invisible Victims

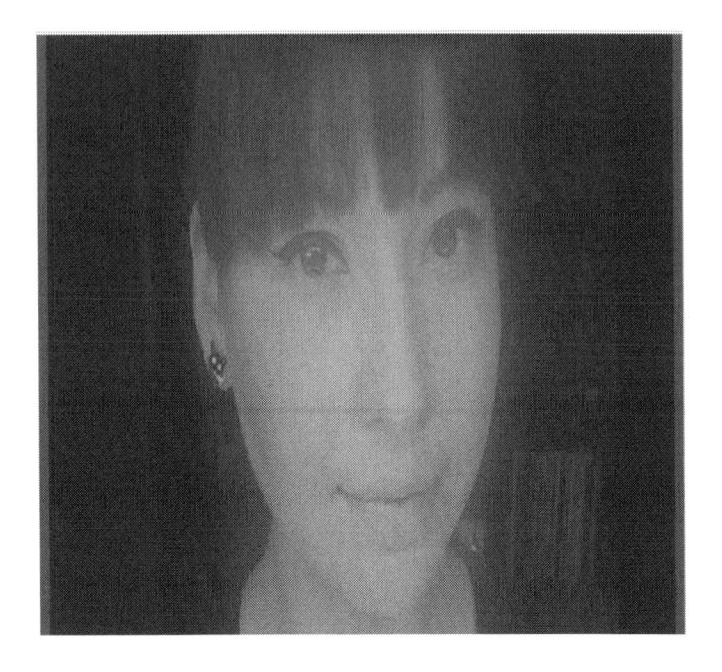

Bella had the world at her feet. Young, talented, extroverted, happy. She was doing exactly what she wanted to do with her life. Drawing on her traditional Sturgeon Lake Cree Nation Cree culture, she found a way to incorporate her creative beadwork talents in the world of contemporary fashion. She attended schools in Alberta and then transferred to Humber College in Toronto in order to complete her degree in Fashion Arts. She had plans to move to London, England next to further her career. While leaving home was a big step for Bella, she knew, to succeed in that industry, she'd have to spend time in the larger fashion centers of the world. And this beautiful spirited soul was on the cusp of realizing all her dreams.

Some assumed that Bella lived a high-risk lifestyle that led to her death. Her family is adamant that this is not the case. Bella came from a very strong family in Northwestern Alberta who fully supported her in realizing her dreams. Her father is the Chief of the Cree Lubicon Lake Band. "Bella was one of the lucky First Nations young people who grew up with both parents in her life who have been together for over 25 years. Her Mom and Dad have been teachers and educators who developed Cree curriculum for language revitalization for the past three decades. Both parents graduated with a Masters in Education. Language and culture was an important part of both their lives, and this was passed on to Bella. On both sides of the family, Bella's grandparents and aunties are cultural knowledge carriers and maintain teachings and practice traditional artwork and beading that Bella continued into her life."[66] A quick look at Bella's tribute page[67] on the community-sponsored website It Starts With Us shows just how well grounded and normal her short life was.

Invisible Victims

To the horror of her beloved family, Bella's death was originally ruled and is still considered merely "suspicious." But not a homicide. So as in the case of Carol King previously discussed, Bella's death would not show up in any of the MMIW reports published by the RCMP or Stats Canada. Appalling is the fact that it was two full weeks before a single story about the tragic and horrible death of Bella Laboucan-McLean appeared in local media.

Katherine McCarthy

Highway of Tears (British Columbia)

In northern British Columbia, a 724-kilometer highway corridor that is part of Highway 16 has been dubbed The Highway of Tears. To some, it is not all that remarkable. There is some attractive greenery surrounding this highway but nothing compared to the other well known areas of the province. It is, for all intents and purposes, just another Canadian highway. However, it is the history associated with this stretch of highway that makes it remarkable. Its legacy is not pleasant. For decades, more than 40 women have gone missing or have been murdered along that stretch of highway. All but one of them were Indigenous.

    The true tragedy behind the Highway of Tears is not just the fact that so many innocent women ended up dead or missing after they were last seen there, or the fact that remains were discovered on it. It is the fact that these murders have been occurring for decades and there has only been one potential suspect. No-one has ever even been close to finding out who is really committing all of these heinous crimes. Ineffective investigations into the Highway of Tears is further seen by the fact that the only primary suspect in the murders was incarcerated in 1995 and there have been more murders since he was locked away.

It has been difficult for investigators to discover any other pattern except that the majority of the victims were Indigenous women. The ages varied from 12 to 33 years old, and it is still unclear if the murders and disappearances along the Highway of Tears were the work of a single serial killer, multiple perpetrators working together, or several random serial killers.

In 2005, the E-PANA Task Force within the RCMP was created with the mandate to investigate three murders along the Highway of Tears that occurred in 1994. These cases were thought to have commonalities by the criminal profilers within the RCMP, and they were also thought to be the possible work of a serial killer. It was then decided that the scope needed to be expanded if they were to consider a serial killer angle.

To be considered an E-PANA case, there were three factors the task force looked at:
- The victim was female,
- The victim was involved in a high-risk activity that exposed them to danger (hitchhiking or involved in street trade/prostitution),

- The victim had to have been last seen or their body found within a mile of three BC highways (Highway 16, 97 or 5).

The task force had 50 investigators with 10 support staff and they were given a $6 million annual budget to solve these cases. In 2006, it took ownership of nine murder cases. After finishing the review of all the potential cases in 2007, the final case load that E-PANA would take on doubled to 18. It has remained the same since. Those 18 MMIW cases include 13 homicides and five missing women. The cases date from 1969 to 2006.[68]

Invisible Victims

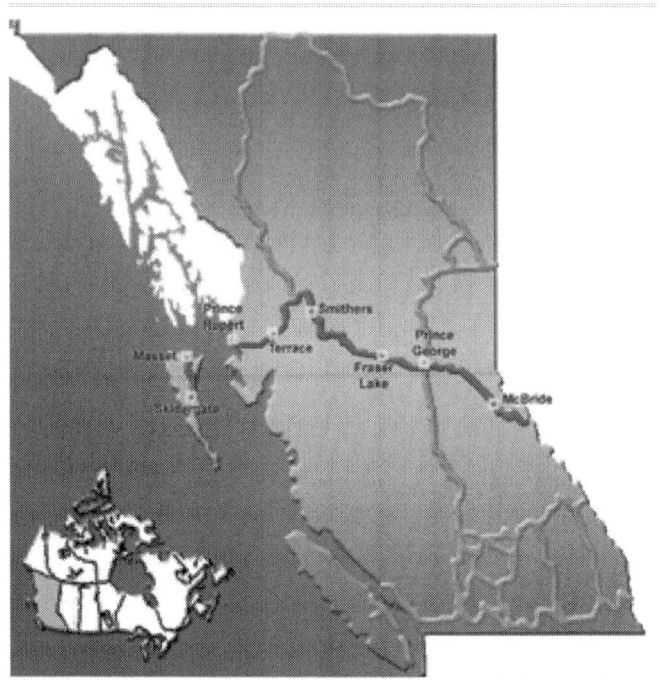

Illustration 1: British Columbia Route 16 aka Highway of Tears

Katherine McCarthy

Illustration 1: Sign displaying Highway of Tears

Victims and Suspects

The E-PANA Task Force case list has become synonymous with the number of Highway of Tears victims. However, human rights groups that focus on the Highway of Tears murders and community grassroots organizations estimate that the number of victims are closer to forty women and girls if not fifty. Below is a list of the cases E-PANA is investigating.

The first known victim was 27-year-old Gloria Moody. She was last seen in October 1969 and disappeared while taking a weekend trip to Williams Lake, BC. Her remains were found in the woods later that month.

The second victim was considerably younger than the first. In 1970, 18-year-old Micheline Pare had been dropped off by two friends thinking she was close enough to where she was going that she would be safe. Her remains were found on August 8 near Hudson's Hope, BC.

There were two murders towards the end of 1973 - one in October and another in November - that occurred between the towns of Clearwater and Kamloops. Both of these cases were the first to which US serial killer and rapist Bobby Jack Fowler, a name that would eventually become famously connected to the Highways of Tears, would become a person of interest.

The first of these two victims was named Gale Weys, 19. Gale was last seen on October 19, 1973, in Clearwater when she left the gas station where she worked. She decided to hitchhike to visit her parents in nearby Kamloops. Her body was found half a year later on April 6, 1974, just south of Clearwater, with clear signs that she had been raped. Over time, DNA evidence would strongly point to Bobby Fowler as the person responsible for her rape and murder; however, this has not yet been proven conclusively.[69]

Just a month after Gale disappeared, 19-year-old Pamela Darlington told her friends that she was going to hitchhike to a nearby bar within the town of Kamloops. Her badly beaten body was found the next day in the Thompson River at Pioneer Park with the same clear signs of sexual trauma that had been found with Gale. Later, DNA evidence collected from her body would lead authorities to strongly suspect Bobby Fowler as the person responsible in Pamela's murder as well.

After a short break of roughly eight months, the Highway of Tears murders legacy

Invisible Victims

returned with a vengeance. Two more murders occurred in the same year within a span of four months. A disturbing trend was now noticeable if all of these women were being murdered by the same individual. The victims ages were steadily decreasing. It seemed as though the perpetrator, if all of the murders were connected, was moving from targeting women to young girls.

The first girl to be murdered in 1974 was 16-year-old Colleen MacMillen. She was last seen in August on Highway 97 near Lac La Hache heading to a friend's house just a few short kilometers away. She had decided to hitchhike the way there. Her remains were found a month later off a logging road 46 kilometers from where she was last seen. Almost forty years later, DNA evidence found on her body decisively implicated Bobby Jack Fowler, making him the prime suspect for other Highway of Tears murders.

The second victim of 1974 came four months after Colleen was found. On December 13, 14-year-old Monica Ignas was abducted and killed while she was going home from school. She was reported missing, but her body was not found until several months later in April 1975, having been raped and strangled to death. Although there has been no DNA evidence recovered that could implicate Bobby

Fowler, it is suspected that he was involved in this murder as well.

The next victim of the Highway of Tears murder legacy is considered perhaps the most tragic out of all of the stories. Monica Jack was only 12 years old when she disappeared on May 6, 1978, while riding her bike near Nicola Lake in the town of Merritt along Highway 5. For 17 years, five years longer than her entire life, Monica's remains were not found. Only her bike was found the day after her disappearance near Swakum Mountain, but Monica's fate was unknown. Then in June of 1995, forestry workers discovered her skeletal remains. It was originally suspected that her murder was also the work of Bobby Fowler, but in 2014, 36 years after Monica's death, a serial killer and rapist named Garry Taylor Handlen was arrested for her murder as well as the murder of another child in Abbotsford, B.C., 11-year-old Kathryn-Mary Herbert.

On May 8, 1981, three years after the death of the youngest victim in the history of the Highway of Tears, 33-year-old Maureen Mosie disappeared while hitchhiking on the Highway of Tears. Her body was found on Highway 97, 16 kilometers east of Kamloops. She was the third victim to be killed in or around that town. However, the killer's MO was different this time, as Maureen had been

Invisible Victims

viciously beaten. A brutality that was not seen in previous murders committed along the Highway of Tears.

Two years after the murder of Maureen, 16-year-old Shelly-Ann Bascu fell victim to the Highway of Tears. Shelly-Ann called her mother on May 3, 1983, at 8 pm to let her know she was on her way home and to ask her mom if she would cook her some pasta. But she didn't show up. Still today, law enforcement officials know nothing of where she might be or who might have abducted her. All that is certain is that Shelly-Ann was accosted violently as articles of her clothing as well as droplets of blood that were confirmed to match her blood type were found near the Athabasca River. Her case has been cold now for over 30 years.

On September 25, 1989, the body of 24-year-old Alberta Williams was found 37 kilometers east of Prince Rupert. Not much is known regarding where she was last seen or her situation before her death, but what is known is that Alberta was strangled and her body showed clear signs of rape.

The next victim of the Highway of Tears was 15-year-old Delphine Nikal. She was last seen hitchhiking east from the town of Smithers on June 13, 1990. Authorities have been unable to locate her body or identify any suspect. Delphine's cousin Cicilia also disappeared without a trace from Vancouver in October the year before and has never been found.

In 1994, three young girls, all aged either 15 or 16 years old, were murdered. The first of these three, 16-year-old Ramona Wilson, was last seen on high school graduation night, June 11, hitchhiking to a friend's place. When she didn't show up later that night, her family put it on the local radio station to tell her to phone home. When her family didn't get a response from her by Monday, they contacted the police to ask them to help the family look for her. They were told they had to wait two more days in case she showed up. Sadly, she didn't. Ramona's remains were found 10 months later near the Smithers airport on April 9. Her case is still unsolved. Ramona is profiled in several documentaries about the Highway of Tears and Missing and Murdered Indigenous Women in Canada such as: "Finding Dawn", "Highway of Tears," and "An Ex-Cop's Mission to Solve the Murders Along the Highway of Tears." Her case is kept alive by her family and friends, but mainly because of the Annual Ramona Wilson Memorial Walk. To deal with the grief and sadness, family and friends get together every year on June 11 and walk the two miles from where she was last seen to where her body was found.

The second victim killed in 1994 was Roxanne Thiara. Roxanne disappeared in July 1994 and reportedly was last seen by a friend who stated she was going to meet a client. Sadly, 15-year-old Roxanne worked in the sex trade. Her body was found the very next month on August 17 just off the Highway of Tears. Her murder is to date unsolved.

The last of the three victims that were murdered in the 1994 rash of killings was 15-year-old Alishia Germaine. Alishia disappeared in December after enjoying a Christmas dinner at the Native Friendship Center in Prince George. Her body was found on the 19th of December outside an elementary school just off of Highway 16. Alishia's murder was different from the others because she was the first of all of the victims to have been stabbed to death.

It is widely suspected that Bobby Fowler had a role to play in these murders similar to the murders of 1973-74. In both instances, the murders were committed in quick succession and targeted mainly hitchhikers. However, no DNA evidence has been uncovered so far that successfully links Fowler to any of these three murders. Bobby Fowler was arrested in the US on June 28, 1995, for kidnapping, attempted rape and coercion, assault and menacing. He was convicted and went to prison in January 1996. He would do no more damage since he died in prison in 2006.

The next victim that fell prey to the Highway of Tears was named Lana Derrick who was a 19-year-old college student at the time of her disappearance. She was visiting her mom in Terrace, BC when she went missing on October 6, 1995. Police say she was last seen at a gas station on Highway 16 near Terrace; however, her mom believes the last place she was seen was her friend Clarice's house. She is still missing.

The next official victim of The Highway of Tears is 25-year-old Nicole Hoar. On June 21, 2002, Nicole disappeared while hitchhiking along Highway 16, west of Prince George. She has never been found. Nicole's case was a turning point in the Highway of Tears murders because, sadly, the media coverage it received compared to the other murders revealed an obvious racial bias present in the media. Nicole was a young white woman, and it was only after her disappearance that the issue in Northern BC started to garner attention, both nationally and internationally. Nicole's disappearance finally prompted authorities to really take the matter seriously – something they just hadn't been doing when the victims had only been young Indigenous women.

Invisible Victims

Three years after Nicole's disappearance, 22-year-old Tamara Lynn Chipman vanished on September 21, 2005. She had last been seen hitchhiking on Highway 16 near Prince Rupert. Sadly, Tamara is still missing and police have no clues about her disappearance. CBC's website for unsolved missing and murdered Indigenous women states that Tamara has a boy who was two and a half when she disappeared. As a fisherman's daughter, she spent lots of time outdoors and grew up with a deep appreciation for the water.[70]

Aielah Saric-Auger was only 14 years old when she disappeared on February 2, 2006. Her family believed she was spending the night at a friend's house; however, she was last spotted outside a bar in Prince George. Her body was found a week later by a motorist along Highway 16 east of Prince George. Sadly, her murder is still unsolved.[71]

Katherine McCarthy

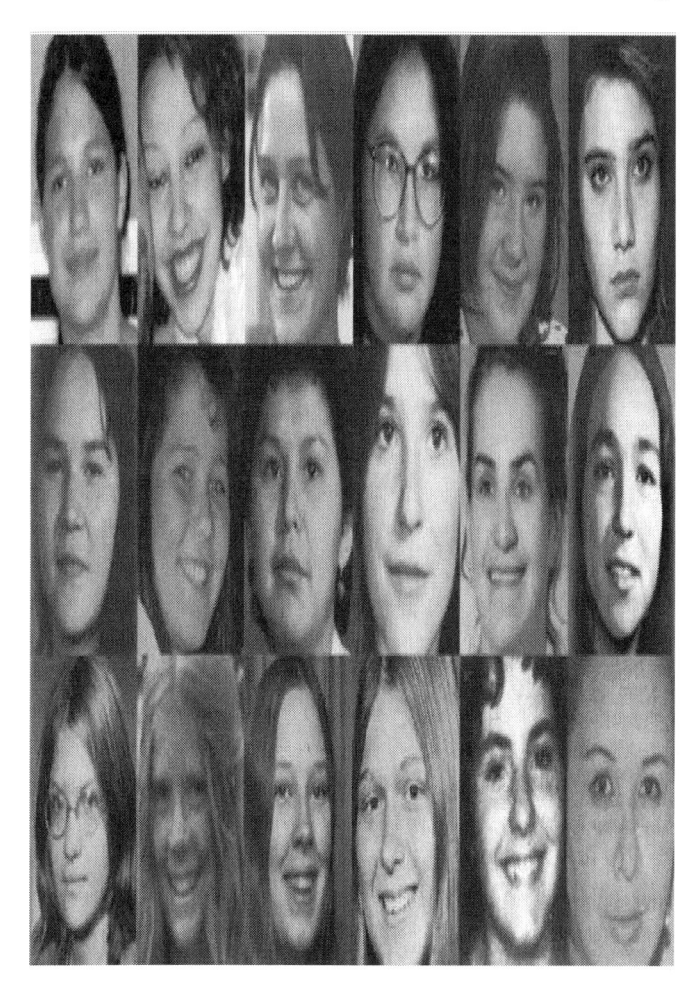

To date, the only real suspect in these 18 Highway of Tears murders was Bobby Jack Fowler. He was the prime suspect in three cases, but law enforcement officials stated that he was most likely the chief perpetrator of as many as ten of these murders and disappearances. This may be unjustified conjecture on their part – an attempt by them to justify their lack of results by claiming that their prime suspect was arrested in the US on an unrelated charge and is now deceased. Thus they are able to close these cases.

The only murder among these 18 in which the perpetrator was successfully apprehended and will pay for his crime is that of the youngest victim, 12-year-old Monica Jack. Her murderer, Garry Handlen, was arrested in December 2014 and is in jail awaiting trial for Monica's murder as well as the murder of 11-year-old Kathryn-Mary Herbert. Strangely enough, E-PANA did not solve Monica's murder even though it was on its list. In 2009, a documentary created for the Canadian Broadcasting Company (CBC) by film maker David Ridgen on the Herbert case showcased the flaws in the investigation, missing documentation and potential suspects of the murder.[72] The documentary prompted the RCMP to take another look at the case with fresh eyes. They did, and after all this time, there was enough evidence to tie Handlen to Kathryn-Mary's murder. The police would not reveal what caused the break in the case, but they are confident they will get a conviction.

In the cases connected to Bobby Fowler, by the time the DNA results could conclusively identify him as Colleen MacMillan's killer or any of the other murders on this list, he was already dead.

If the police want to really catch the serial killers in Canada, isn't it time to widen the scope of this project? Other murders have occurred in Northern BC, and the province of BC has the highest number of missing and murdered Indigenous women in Canada. There are several right in Prince George actually. However, because they didn't occur technically on one of those three highways, they were excluded from E-PANA. For instance, 38-year-old Theresa Umphrey who was murdered by Brian Arp in Prince George; 35-year-old Jill Stuchenko, 35 year old Cynthia Maas, and 23-year-old Natasha Montgomery who was killed by serial killer Cody Legebekoff in Prince George.

Out of all 18 of these murders and disappearances, the only one that really seemed to make any headlines in the media was the disappearance of Nicole Hoar. People in BC and the rest of Canada were shocked to hear that women were going missing and being murdered in northern BC and no-one heard a word of it in the news. While glad of the sudden interest from the media, Indigenous groups were also rightfully upset. It was painfully obvious that people truly only started caring about the Highway of Tears murders because of Nicole, because of the fact that Nicole was a white woman who fell prey to the Highway's brutal legacy. It demonstrated evidence of systemic racism that has become endemic to the institutions of law enforcement and the media in Canada.

Anna Mae Pictou (NS & USA)

On a cold night in December in South Dakota, 30-year-old Annie Mae Pictou stumbled up an embankment on the edge of the Pine Ridge Indian Reservation knowing this would be the final leg of her death march. Beaten, bruised and hurting all over from the past 72 hours of interrogation, she found the courage to try and reason with her captors and make them believe she was not an FBI Informant. She knew it was useless. Her final request was to ask if she could pray before they ended her life, and as she knelt, she thought of her young daughters. The last thing she heard was the cocking of the revolver. Then finally the blast. Shot at close range in the back of the head, she was barely alive as she fell 30 feet into a ravine. Finally she was alone. As she lay there in her final moments, she curled into a fetal position and said her final prayers to the Creator for her daughters and loved ones to be safe and to remember all she had taught them.

Invisible Victims

Annie Mae Pictou was born on March 27, 1945, and raised on the Mi'kmaq Indian Brook Reserve in Shubenacadie, Nova Scotia. Growing up amid racism and poverty, Annie Mae moved to the US to find a better life. Deeply affected by her own experience with racism and oppression, she bore a fiery devotion towards Indigenous rights. She wanted to become an activist against the brutal injustices towards the Indigenous people in Canada and the US. Hundreds of years of subjugation left a lot of disenfranchisement and inter-generational trauma for her people. She believed she could make a difference. She believed she could bring back traditional cultural values and sense of honor to the people and regain what had been stolen from them. She believed in creating a better world for her children and other children. She wanted to fight for environment issues. So she became a warrior.

Annie Mae moved to the New England area of the US to work as a harvester, as was common among the Mi'kmaq people, then to the city of Boston when she was still only 17 years old. There she married Jake Maloney and had two daughters. She kept strong ties to Canada as the family moved back and forth between Nova Scotia and Boston for years. While employed in a factory in 1968, she found time to volunteer in Boston's Indian Council helping urban Indigenous youth develop self-esteem as a way to help them resist drug and alcohol abuse that was so common at the time. She learned about the American Indian Movement (AIM) while volunteering at the Council. Believing it to be just the solution she was looking for to bring about positive and great change for the Indigenous people, she joined and started fighting for Indigenous rights. In 1973, she married Nogeeshik Aquash, a Chippewa artist from Ontario. Together they became involved in the growing Indian rights movement. They participated in many of AIM's civil rights initiatives, including the 71-day armed occupation of Wounded Knee in 1973. This occupation was actually a standoff between the residents of Pine Ridge Indian Reservation and the federal government (FBI, National Guard and US Marshal Service) over the corrupt running of the reservation and a failure of government to fulfill treaty obligations. That site was chosen by AIM because of its painful historical significance to the 1890 Wounded Knee slaughter of 300 native men, women and children by US Calvary. Upon meeting Dennis Banks, founder of AIM at Wounded Knee, Banks told her that newcomers were needed on kitchen duty. "Mr. Banks," Annie Mae replied, "I didn't come here to wash dishes. I came here to fight."[73] The standoff ended after two Native Americans died and 13 were wounded. One hundred eighty-five indictments were handed down. The Aquashes moved back to Boston after Wounded Knee but continued to work for the movement. In 1974, Annie Mae moved to St. Paul, Minnesota, to work full time at AIM's head office. Her work with the movement there put her on the FBI's radar.

Standing only 5' 2", Annie Mae was small, but her presence was powerful. She became very important to the movement. She was running a cultural school in Minneapolis, was integral to the fund-raising efforts for the organization, and was privy to the decisions made among the leadership. For a long time she was a well-respected member of AIM – with the exception of the 'Pie Patrol'. The Pie Patrol was a group of women within AIM that kept a strict eye on the social happenings and stepped in if one of the women did something they felt was inappropriate. Among its few members were the wives, sisters and close friends of the leaders. They didn't care for Annie Mae. Smart, outspoken and moving quickly up the ranks, they probably felt threatened by this newcomer.

Over time, the actions of AIM became more and more radical. She spoke up often in opposition about the direction they were taking and became unpopular because of it. In early 1975, things drastically changed within AIM, bringing with it major changes for Annie Mae. With all radical anti-government groups, there was a risk of being infiltrated with government informants. AIM was no exception. Over the years, many lower level operatives were uncovered as spies. However, when Douglass Durhan came out as an FBI informant, it shook AIM's foundations. He had managed to work his way up to head of their security. Extreme paranoia followed this revelation. Very few were trusted after that – especially not an outsider from another country with no Lakota family ties to the organization or the reservation. After Annie Mae was released on bond a little too quickly after being arrested a few times, and coincidentally people were getting arrested more often when she was around, rumors started to emerge among the members that she was an informant. What they didn't realize was that because she was important to the fund-raising efforts of the organization, and the fact that she was for a brief time romantically involved with one of its leaders, Dennis Banks, her bail was usually arranged faster than most other people's. And it is true that she was asked by the FBI to be an informant. They were most eager to find out whatever they could about the murder of two of their agents in June that year. But she refused. Still the rumors were spreading rapidly.

In June of 1975, the rumors of Annie Mae being an Informant for the government had reached the melting point. At the annual AIM convention in New Mexico that month, Leonard Peltier, Dennis Banks's bodyguard, and Bob Robideaux interrogated her. They were determined to find out if she was an informant or not. It was said that he threatened her with a gun during this interrogation by putting it in her mouth or to her head. She bravely told them that if they really thought that was true, to go ahead and kill her now. She convinced them for a time anyway. However, from then on, she never went anywhere alone and was constantly watched. Shortly after the convention, two FBI agents named Coler and Williams were following someone they believed to be a fugitive. They found themselves driving into a place called Jumping Bull on the Pine Ridge Indian Reservation. A shootout occurred and they were both shot and killed. Tensions between the FBI and AIM were immensely escalated at this point. Leonard Peltier was found guilty of their murders and is still serving out two life sentences.

In early fall, Annie Mae managed to make a trip back to Canada to see her family. She told her sister about AIM's suspicions and her interrogation. Obviously, her sister didn't want her to go back and begged her not to, realizing the danger she was in. However, Annie Mae was stubborn and she wanted to convince them of her innocence. She also spoke of all the good people in the movement and that the work they were doing was making a difference. She had to make sure those she cared about knew she wasn't an informant. So she went back to South Dakota.

After being arrested and charged with having weapons in September 1975, she was again let go rather quickly, causing even more suspicion. Then again in October, she was driving in a motorhome with Dennis Banks, Leonard Peltier, KaMook Banks and others when a highway patrolman happened to pull them over. All the occupants got out of the motorhome except for Banks. He drove off, leaving his pregnant wife, his mistress and all the others. Peltier also got away. The rest were arrested and Annie Mae was held for a while this time for outstanding warrant.

When she appeared in court on November 24, the judge let her out on bond yet again. It is unknown if law enforcement knew or understood the impact that this lenient treatment of Annie Mae would have. KaMook Banks testified at Arlo Looking Cloud's trial[74] that during their time in the motorhome, Annie Mae, KaMook and others witnessed Leonard Peltier bragging about killing the FBI agents and how one was begging for his life but he killed him anyway. A combination of Annie Mae having that knowledge, along with an awareness of other past and future misdeeds, and a growing consensus that she was a fed, sadly sealed her fate.

In early December of that year, she was interrogated again. Only this time it wasn't so much an interrogation as it was a death march. Over a period of three days, Annie Mae was kidnapped, dragged from city to city, house to house, questioned repeatedly, beaten, raped, murdered execution style, and finally left for dead by members of AIM. This was from the testimony and accounts of many eyewitnesses, many of them AIM members.

On February 24, 1976, an unusual thaw led to the discovery of a woman's remains at the bottom of a ravine on the outskirts of the Pine Ridge Indian Reservation. A local rancher found the body while riding the perimeter of his property. The decomposed state of 'Jane Doe' only revealed she had been there a while. During the first autopsy, the X-ray machine was broken, which led to the coroner missing the fact that Jane Doe was shot in the head. He concluded that the cause of death was exposure. He was also unable to get fingerprints due to the advanced rate of decomposition. Standard protocol in this case was to remove the hands and send them to the FBI's lab where they could perform fingerprinting analysis with more advanced technology. Despite orders to wait for an ID before burying Jane Doe, she was interred on March 2, 1976. A week later, the fingerprint analysis revealed Jane Doe to be the missing Annie Mae Pictou Aquash, one of the FBI's most wanted. Her family in Canada was notified, and they quickly requested a second autopsy as they suspected foul play. At the same time, the FBI was in the process of ordering a second autopsy as well. Strangely enough, her family and friends at AIM did not want a second autopsy. They said it would just 'cause trouble' when it was discussed with the family. On March 11, Annie Mae's body was exhumed and a different medical examiner, Dr. Gary Peterson, conducted a second autopsy. The bullet was found and the cause of death was concluded to be a gunshot wound to the head.

The death of Annie Mae caused extreme fear among the members of AIM. Investigators couldn't get anyone to talk about her murder. They interviewed over 200 people about her death. Not one person would agree to speak out. AIM leaders quickly blamed the feds for her murder, arguing they did it to create dissension and fear within AIM. At the same time, they painted Annie Mae as a hero of the movement. The members of AIM wanted to believe this to be true and chose to believe it. For almost twenty years, her family knew nothing. Her children only knew that she died fighting for her people. no-one from AIM contacted them during this time, but they did hear through the grapevine that it was the FBI that was responsible for her death.

What they didn't know was that a small handful of people pressed on over the years, haunted by her death and struggling to find the real truth. If not for the tenacity of a few individuals, the justice that was eventually found would not have been. Between 1976 and 1999, four grand juries took up the case without any arrests. There was just not enough evidence. Then an unlikely witness, Darlene KaMook Nicols, stepped up in 1999. She was an unlikely witness because she was Dennis Banks's ex-wife and was still with him at the time Banks and Annie Mae were having an affair. She also had four children with Banks. Regardless, she still considered Annie Mae a friend and desired the truth to come out. Courageously, over the next year, she secretly recorded conversations with ten witnesses that could account for Annie Mae's final days. The trail led her to Arlo Looking Cloud, a low-level AIM member in 1975, who was there throughout Annie Mae's 72-hour death march and witnessed her murder. He eventually confessed all to law enforcement and, in 2003, was charged with first degree murder. He also testified against John Graham, the gunman. In 2004, Looking Cloud was found guilty and received a life sentence that was later reduced to 20 years[75] in 2011. John Graham was charged at the same time as Looking Cloud; however, he was not tried until 2010. It took six years to get him extradited from Canada to stand trial. Two courts ruled that the U.S. lacked jurisdiction to try him because he was not an American Indian.[76] However, once the federal courts made their ruling, the state was right there and ready to pick up the case. He pled not guilty but was convicted and sentenced to life. A third abductor, Theda Nelson Clarke, was never charged since she was 80 years old by this time and living in a nursing home. She died in October 2011 at the age of 87. A fourth person, Richard Marshall, was charged with aiding and abetting for providing the gun that was used to kill Annie Mae; however, he was found not guilty. Finally a fifth person, Thelma Rios, was charged for her role in the murder. She allowed the trio of kidnappers to hold Annie Mae at her house in Rapid City. She was also the person who relayed the message for them to bring Annie Mae back from Denver to Rapid City because they determined she was a government informant. She pled guilty as an accessory to kidnapping and was sentenced to five years in prison. That was later suspended to five years' probation. She also died in 2011.

Despite all these charges, trials and convictions, this case still isn't over. Annie Mae was pretty high up in the ranks of AIM. The low-level positions of the people who kidnapped and executed her would not have done it without being ordered to do so. Those charged and convicted were soldiers, not decision makers. To date, no AIM leader has been charged with ordering her slaying, though lots of finger pointing has happened over the years. In November 1999, Russell Means publicly accused Vernon and Clyde Bellecourt in a press conference of ordering her death. Vernon Bellecourt was an AIM Leader and Head of Security and Intelligence at the time of Annie Mae's murder. Means stated in his press conference that he believed they ordered her murder because they falsely believed she was an informant and that she was going to provide testimony about the murder of the two FBI agents that Leonard Peltier was in prison for. The next day, Vernon publicly denied the accusation and suggested that it was Means himself who was involved. Vernon Bellecourt died in 2007.

Investigators have even tried getting the Pie Patrol to implicate who ordered the murder, offering them immunity in exchange for their testimony. They refused. Dennis Banks denies any involvement, yet both his ex-wife, KaMook, and former spokesperson for AIM, John Trudell, testified under oath that Banks told them about Annie Mae's death before her body was even officially identified by authorities. KaMook remembers it was February 24 when Dennis called and told her they had found Annie Mae's body. She remembers the date exactly because she was sitting at a desk and she looked at the calendar. It was her nephew's birthday and she made a mental note to call him later. However, Annie Mae's body was not identified until March 3rd. As well, John Trudell testified at another AIM trial (Robideaux and Butler) in June 1976 that Dennis Banks told him about Annie Mae on February 25 or 26. More specifically, he was told by Banks that she was found and she was shot in the back of the head.[77] Again, this was before she was officially identified on March 3 and also before the second autopsy on March 10 when the bullet was found. So how did he know it was Annie Mae that was found? And how did he know that she was shot in the head? A better question yet is why has Banks not been forced to answer that question. Technically, it's still an open case, so there's still hope that those truly responsible for her death will be held accountable. In the words of Annie Mae's own daughter, Denise, "regardless how long ago it happened, justice is justice."

Invisible Victims

Katherine McCarthy

Serial Killers

After the release of the RCMP report on MMIW in 2014, and Bernard Valcout's comment that 70 percent of all murdered Indigenous women were, in fact, killed by Indigenous men, the shock waves and rage were felt throughout all First Nations communities in Canada. And rightfully so. The comment was seen as a blatant attempt to 'pass the buck' and blame the crisis on family violence, or to take the pressure off law enforcement agencies in Canada for their mishandling of Indigenous people's cases. Indigenous communities knew this to be untrue, but unfortunately, the general public did not. Some now know the difference. With more and more information surfacing, the general public is becoming more aware and mistrusting of what we are being told by our government, law enforcement, and the media.

The Globe and Mail is creating its own database of MMIWs starting with the NWAC database, adding work done by researcher Maryann Pearce. They estimate that 20 percent of serial killer victims in Canada since 1980 were Indigenous women[78] and can list 18 victims. With their project, "if the scope is broadened to include cases with a probable suspect…,then the number rises to about 35. And if the scope is further expanded to include speculative cases, for which court proceedings are pending or police have said a serial killer may be at work, the number rises dramatically, to about 77."[79] As mentioned previously, *The Toronto Star* estimated that 13 percent of Indigenous women are killed by serial killers.

Why would serial killers target Indigenous women in Canada? The answer to this question is easy. They are less likely to be undercover cops, they pick up on the general public's apathy that no-one would care, it is generally known that the police aren't as diligent in solving these cases, and the media doesn't make as big of a deal as when non-Indigenous women are murdered.

Along with the Canadian serial killers apprehended and tried in Canada, there were a few US-based ones investigated for the murders in Vancouver's Downtown Eastside as well -- Gary Ridgway: Green River Killer, Dayton Leroy Rogers: Molalla Forest Killer, Keith Hunter Jespersen: The Happy Face Killer, Robert Yates (convicted of killing thirteen prostitutes in nearby Seattle), and Ronald Richard McCauley.[80]

Cody Alan Legebekoff

Cody Legebekoff is Canada's second youngest serial killer. At the tender age of 19, a year after he graduated high school, Legebekoff brutally killed his first victim. By pure luck alone, 14 months later, he was captured immediately after killing his last victim, a 15-year-old free spirit he met online. A year later, DNA evidence found in his apartment would tie him to three more murders in Prince George, BC. At 24 years old, Legebekoff was convicted of killing three women and one teenage girl -- Jill Stuchenko and Cynthia Maas, both 35, Natasha Montgomery, 23, and 15-year-old Loren Leslie. To date, these are the murders that law enforcement has tied to him; however, there seems to be almost a year-long gap between the first murder and the other three. Two of his victims were Indigenous women living in Prince George.

Experts claim his modus operandi (MO) was "...to target vulnerable women, sexually assault them and then kill them by inflicting massive facial and upper body blunt-force trauma and sharp-force trauma using various tools and implements."[81] Jill disappeared on October 9, 2009, and her body was found on the 20th of that same month partially buried in a gravel pit. The murders of Natasha, Cynthia and Loren all occurred within a three-month span. Natasha went missing on September 1, 2010, but her body has yet to be found. Cynthia went missing the very next week on September 10 and her remains were found October 9. Just a short time later, on November 27, Legebekoff was pulled over for speeding out of a logging road and, thanks to the diligence of a rookie cop, was not long afterward arrested for the murder of Loren.

Even though Legebekoff is currently serving 25 years for each of the four murders, unfortunately, the Canadian justice system states that each 25-year sentence will be served concurrently, or at the same time. As well, the clock started ticking on his jail time when he was arrested in November 2010. He was just 20 years old at the time. Shockingly, this means that Legebekoff will be eligible for parole when he is 45 years old. If that isn't bad enough, Canada's 'faint hope clause' allows Legebekoff to apply for early parole after serving just 15 of those years. Even though the 'faint hope clause' was repealed in 2011 for multiple murderers, Legebokoff's crimes occurred before then, so this clause is available to him. It is entirely possible that Legebekoff could be walking the streets again a free man when he is 35 years old.

Bestselling author JT Hunter expertly recounts his story, including details of his crimes, Legebokoff's interrogation and trial in Volume 6 of the Crimes Canada series, *The Country Boy Killer: The True Story of Cody Legebekoff*.

Invisible Victims

According to Hunter, Legebekoff "was the friendly, baby-faced, Canadian boy next door. He came from a loving, caring, and well respected family. Blessed with good looks and back-woods country charm, he was popular with his peers, and although an accident at birth left permanent nerve damage in one of his arms, he excelled in sports. A self-proclaimed 'die hard' Calgary Flames fan, he played competitive junior hockey and competed on his school's snowboarding team. And he enjoyed the typical simple pleasures of a boy growing up in the country: camping, hunting, and fishing with family and friends. But he also enjoyed brutally murdering women, and he would become one of the youngest serial killers in Canadian history." Legebekoff was completely unknown to police. A friendly high-school jock supposedly raised by a good family in Fort St. James, Legebekoff grew up hunting and fishing with his grandfather. He had a girlfriend, a steady job at a car dealership and plans for the future. A typical 'country boy', he wasn't on anyone's radar. So when he was arrested for the murder of Loren Leslie, everyone was shocked. Shock gave way to horror when DNA evidence tied him to three more murders a year later.

Serial killers usually exhibit some early signs of trouble. Behavioral specialists refer to them as the Triad -- animal torture, fire setting, and bed wetting past the age of twelve. They often experience mental or physical trauma growing up.[82] It is unknown whether Legebekoff experienced any of these early signs. Neither he nor his family would talk. I said above that a good family 'supposedly' raised him. However, we don't really know that for sure. Aside from one statement from his grandfather about their fishing expeditions, the rest of his family has never been interviewed, and they were curiously absent during the entire trial. Loren Leslie's mother actually reached out and called Legebokoff's family at one point in an effort to deal with her grief; however, she was told to never call there again.[83] Legebekoff had moved away from his hometown to the larger city of Prince George, and his friends told the media that he had been doing a lot of crack cocaine around the time of the murders.

As most serial killers, Legebekoff was completely devoid of any emotion or remorse during his interrogation and especially the trial. His explanation of events was riddled with lies. When he was pulled over by a rookie cop for speeding immediately after bludgeoning Loren Leslie to death, he explained with an eerie calmness that the blood all over him belonged to a deer he'd recently killed. During interviews with police after he was arrested, Legebekoff changed his story several times. Initially, he said he stumbled across Loren's body but had nothing to do with her murder. Once he realized the police were aware that he knew the victim personally, he changed his story. He first denied having sex with the 15 year old. But when told she was found naked from the waist down, he admitted to having sex with her but insisted it was consensual.

A text message found on Loren's phone proved that she had no intention of having sex with him. They were just going to meet up after talking for several weeks online. He then alleged and later testified that Loren 'freaked out' after they had sex and was trying to kill herself by hitting herself with a pipe wrench that was in his truck, and stabbing herself in the neck with a knife. He admitted to hitting her with the pipe but, in his opinion, it was really the same as a mercy killing or putting her out of her misery. At the trial, he admitted to being present when three of the women (Jill, Cynthia and Natasha) were killed. However, he insisted he didn't do the killing. He argued that three other men, drug dealers, killed the women while he only provided the weapons. Refusing to be labeled a 'rat' before going to prison, he would not give their names but referred to them as X, Y and Z. The alphabet theory. No forensic evidence was ever found to support that anyone else was involved in the murders that occurred in his apartment besides him.

On the stand, Legebokoff's lawyer attempted to draw out some emotion from his client on many separate occasions by asking him direct questions about how he was feeling emotionally at the time, or how certain things made him feel. His responses were either "nothing" or some utterance that lacked any emotion. His curt, emotionless responses and testimony did nothing to help his case. Witnesses in the courtroom shivered, including the jury. After his disastrous testimony, his lawyer must have known the jury would convict, so prior to summations, he attempted to make a deal with prosecutors whereby Legebekoff would plead guilty to second degree murder. They refused the deal. They were most confident they would get a conviction. And they did. It only took the jury a day and a half to unanimously decide his guilt in all four of the first degree murder charges. When giving his instructions to the jury, the judge told the jury they could take his late attempt at a plea bargain as an admission of guilt. With a cracking and emotional voice, the judge had some harsh things to say to Legebekoff during his sentencing. "These are not the actions of a simple killer but something infinitely worse. This is a man who by his actions has demonstrated the absolute need to be separated from society, to protect members of that society and, particularly, the most vulnerable of that society who he has targeted."[84]

What stuck me about his testimony and interview with the police was the fact that Legebekoff seemed to have people categorized and separated in his mind. They were either good or bad. The good were to be respected, the bad could be used and discarded. He insisted to police many times that he was just a regular guy and completely normal. Yet he seemed to be obsessed with sex. He insisted he was not the type of guy that would pick up 'hookers'.

Yet he had sex with sex trade workers and practically bragged about the number of women he had been sexual with. When it came to women, to him they were either virgins or whores. The sex trade workers or the ones he met online who took the risk to go out and meet a stranger were expendable. When he spoke of his girlfriend, he said she was different from other women and that he had found a 'good one that he could settle down with'.

In the media, the three women, Jill, Cynthia and Natasha, were often only portrayed as drug addicts and sex trade workers. But does that make them bad people like Cody Legebekoff thought? Those women were people. Real people. They absolutely had their share of troubles, but they also had family and friends that loved them very much. They were sisters, aunts, mothers and loved ones. The families of those women were at the trial every day and found the courage to listen to the gruesome and horrible details of how a person they loved spent their final moments. Whereas the family of Legebekoff didn't come close to the courthouse.

Jill was a talented singer who dreamed of being famous one day. Her friends described her as happy and bubbly. She had six children who will have to live with what happened to their mother. Her 15-year-old daughter's victim impact statement given four years after her mother went missing expressed sorrow that she cried herself to sleep every night. Her good friend testified that just days prior to her going missing, he brought her to a rehab centre to enrol in a program. She really wanted to get off drugs and was serious about getting her children back.[85] Judy Maas, Cynthia Maas's sister, said that "Cindy was a person who saw the good in people, not the evil, she often had sleep overs with her nieces to give them each special attention because family was her first priority. She truly believed life was about having a voice. Despite the struggles that eventually led Cindy to the streets, she'd wanted to change her life. Even though her family was there to help and support her, Cindy was independent and wanted to do that on her own."[86] Cindy overcame great odds to finish school. She had plans to make something of her life. However, she was innocent and trusting, according to her sister. Even when she went to work on the streets, she kept in touch with her family and attended AA meetings. Every day at the courthouse, her sister carried an eagle feather for strength. Extroverted and athletic, Natasha was a figure skater for years and played softball during high school before graduating. "She liked to draw, scrap booking, played the clarinet and trumpet, she liked to sing and do many types of crafts," her mother said. "On family camping trips, Natasha Montgomery enjoyed fishing, tubing, hiking and quadding. It's something we now do in her honor at that special spot where we all liked to get together."[87] Natasha had two children that will have to live with what happened to their mother.

Robert Pickton

Robert Pickton is one of Canada's most notorious serial killers, which is no mean feat in a country so prone to the violence of serial killers, particularly against Canadian Indigenous women. His crimes are particularly famous simply because of the wanton fashion in which they were murdered and disposed of as well as the apathy displayed by the police department of Vancouver while investigating these murders.[88] Bestselling true crime author Chris Swinney does a great job at recounting the details of Pickton's crimes, as well as the Vancouver Police Department and later the RCMP's less than stellar performance in "*The Pig Farmer Killer*,"[89] Volume 1 in this Crimes Canada series.

Invisible Victims

Pickton was well known for hosting wild parties in his slaughterhouse, which would attract hundreds of people. Sex trade workers were a huge part of practically all of his events, and these sex trade workers eventually became his prey when he began his long career as a serial killer. The majority of his victims were Indigenous women. Pickton was a wealthy man after selling some of the family's land for over $5 million in the mid-1990s. This enabled him to easily lure the women to his farm with promises of drugs and alcohol. The first altercation, which eventually came to be seen as a sign of things to come, involved Pickton getting into a fight with a sex trade worker. He attempted to kill her, stabbing her several times before she was able to stab him with his own weapon. He was charged with attempted murder, but the charges were dropped and Pickton gained his freedom with the help of a $2,000 bond.

As the parties continued, a man that was employed as a worker on the farm named Bill Hiscox began to notice that there was a discrepancy between the number of sex trade workers that arrived to attend the party and the number of girls that left the next day. He noticed that some of the girls that visited the farm just never left. Hiscox relayed his suspicions to the law enforcement agencies that executed a warrant for illegal weapons and searched the premises of Pickton's farm. They were quick to jump on the opportunity because a large number of girls had gone missing in recent times from Vancouver's Downtown Eastside and the police force was desperate for any kind of lead.

As luck would have it, an illegal firearm was found which allowed the police officers to take Pickton and his brother into custody. Upon doing so, law enforcement officers obtained a second warrant which allowed them to search the premises again for any clues relating to the sex trade workers that have gone missing. They justified this warrant by informing the judge that an informant had provided them with a tip that led them to believe that searching the premises would allow them to make some major headway in British Columbia's Missing Women List.

Once this second warrant to search the premises had been obtained, the inevitable happened fairly quickly. A rookie police officer stumbled upon an inhaler, which he felt was out of place among the debris that was Pickton's office. This inhaler turned out to belong to Sereena Abotsway, one of the girls that had recently gone missing.

The discovery of the inhaler ended up giving the investigation just the little push it needed. The same rookie police officer discovered an entire bag full of mementos and souvenirs that Pickton had kept to remind him of the murders whenever he felt like reliving them. The acquiring of small, seemingly insignificant items from one's victims is a major part of a serial killer's modus operandi and is usually done because the serial killer wants to keep reliving the event just to be able to feel that way again during a cooling-off period between kills.

Even though Pickton was already in custody for three different charges related to illegal possession of a firearm, he was released. The discovery of the souvenirs allowed the police department to keep him under surveillance. Within the span of a few weeks, he was arrested for the murder of Sereena Abotsway, the girl whose inhaler started it all, and, as DNA evidence continued to pile up, more and more murder convictions were added. Towards the end of his trial, Pickton was being charged with twenty-seven counts of murder in the first degree.

Several years before Pickton was finally arrested, Vancouver's police department received a chilling anonymous tip regarding Pickton's farm. The tip claimed that if the police were to go to Pickton's farm and go through his freezer, they would find that it was full of human meat. Though police officers did go to check the validity of the anonymous claim, and even though Pickton agreed to allow those police officers to search his farm, for some unknown reason, some odd twist of fate, these police officers chose to let it slide. They chose not to search the farm. These two police officers could have prevented dozens of needless deaths.

A chilling aspect of Pickton's modus operandi that resulted in the gradual revealing of the actual victim count was the way he disposed of the bodies of the people he killed.

Pickton would feed the bodies of his victims to his pigs. It was unknown at the time whether Pickton had done this intentionally in order to destroy evidence or whether he was simply just disposing of them at random locations throughout his land where one of his pigs would eventually eat it of their own accord. Whether the act had been intentional or accidental, the fact remained that there was an enormous amount of evidence that was just gone, destroyed by the pigs, dirt and decomposition in general.

    Despite the fact that Pickton was definitely going to jail, the police department of Vancouver still had more than twenty women on the Missing Women's List that were unaccounted for. Twenty women whose remains weren't found at Pickton's farm. In an attempt to discover the truth behind these disappearances, an undercover police officer was put in the cell with Pickton with instructions to find out exactly how many women he had killed. This undercover police officer was placed in the cell before Pickton arrived at the prison to await his next trial date. Armed with a good understanding of Pickton's psychological frame of mind and through clever manipulation, the undercover officer managed to get into the killer's good books very quickly. It was only a matter of time before

Katherine McCarthy

Pickton told the officer what he wanted to know.

A lot of serial killers enjoy boasting about their deeds. Pickton was no exception. Eventually, Pickton told the undercover officer that he had killed forty-nine women. He also told him that he had wanted to kill one more woman to take his kill count up to an even fifty. But he, in his own words, "got sloppy" before he was able to do that. As a result of this undercover officer's excellent work, the police department got to know exactly where those girls went, although the confession that the undercover officer had so skilfully extracted was inadmissible in court. Pickton possesses the classic serial killer mentality. He is arrogant and possesses absolutely no regard for any fellow human beings and, as a result, feels no remorse for what he's done. This sociopathic lack of remorse could be seen throughout his trial as he had his lawyers lodge appeal after appeal and constantly maintained his innocence.

As the trial began, several problems began to emerge with the evidence. It took upwards of a year to finally decide exactly what evidence could be presented for the jury. When the evidence was decided, the judge presiding over the case decided to reject one of the murder charges due to a lack of sufficiently credible and admissible evidence. This brought the total number of charges down to 26. Additionally, the judge deemed it necessary to split the charges into two groups. The first group would include six charges whereas the second group would include the other twenty. The judge did this in order to ensure that no undue stress was placed upon the jury. Involving the jury in a trial that involved twenty-six charges would bind them to a trial that would probably last upwards of two years. Such trials often end in mistrials, which would have resulted in a dangerous serial killer roaming free. Hence, the judge decided to split the charges in order to ensure that a conviction would be made.

Eventually, all of the brutal and gory evidence was finally brought to the courtroom. The jury was so shocked that a member of their community would do something like this that one of the jurors was even accused of having already decided Pickton's innocence. As a result of this bias, the jury returned the verdict that Pickton was not guilty of six counts of murder in the first degree but was guilty of six counts of murder in the second degree.

There are so many disturbing facts regarding the case of Robert Pickton. He intentionally targeted Indigenous women, particularly sex trade workers. The ones he thought no-one would care if they were missing. But perhaps the most disturbing fact is that the jury at his trial declared him not guilty of first degree murder. One of the most prolific serial killers in Canadian history, the man who single-handedly killed dozens of Indigenous women, was declared innocent of first degree murder. He was instead declared guilty of second degree murder. I guess one is only as guilty as the victims are innocent.

26 WOMEN, ONE MAN CHARGED IN THEIR DEATHS

Gilbert Paul Jordan

Gilbert Paul Jordan was a Canadian serial killer active in the province of British Columbia, dubbed "The Alcohol Murders" or "The Boozing Barber" in the media since he was the first Canadian to use alcohol as a murder weapon. He ruthlessly targeted the sex trade workers and downtrodden in Vancouver's Downtown Eastside (DTES), lured them to a hotel or his barber shop with promises of alcohol, then sexually assaulted and killed them after they passed out by pouring more alcohol down their throats until they died. The majority of those he targeted were Indigenous women. He has been linked to the deaths of 8 to 10 women; however, he only served time for the manslaughter conviction of one – a brief six years for the taking of a life.

The Alcohol Murders were very important in the overall history of violence against Indigenous women in Canada. They demonstrated a complete lack of interest from law enforcement. This was evident from a lack of effort in the investigations of missing and murdered Indigenous women to the ridiculously light sentence given to this serial killer.

True crime author Harriet Fox gives a most excellent account in "**The Alcohol Murders: The True Story of Gilbert Paul Jordan,**"[90] Volume 10 of the Crimes Canada Series. The following is just a brief overview of his crimes.

Gilbert Paul Jordan led a very long life of crime. For over 50 years, he plagued the justice system with his criminal deeds that included charges for theft, assaults, drug possession, drunk driving, abduction, rape, hit

Invisible Victims

and run, murder, and more. He was dubbed the town drunk. A loner, withdrawn and antisocial, Jordan only found solace in the company of the women in DTES. As a teenager, his crimes were more along the lines of theft, assaults and drug possession. At 18, he received a one-year sentence for stealing a car. By 21, he had graduated to rape, indecent assault, abduction, hit-and-run, and drunk driving. In 1961, at age 30, he abducted a 5-year-old girl from Mission Indian Reserve in BC. The details of this abduction are unknown. All that is known is that he was arrested, charged with abduction but later acquitted. Months later, he picked up two women from DTES and drove them to Coal Harbour where they consumed vodka. When one of the women stepped out of the car, he drove off, leaving her stranded. He took the other woman to another location where an alleged rape took place. He was charged with rape and theft but was later acquitted of the rape. He was found guilty of theft and sentenced to two years. He appealed the conviction and won. Jordan again walked away free.

He committed his first murder in 1965, at age 34, in a modus operandi (MO) that would soon become notoriously associated with him. A woman named Ivy Rose Oswald was found dead after a night of binge drinking with

Jordan. Her blood alcohol level was an incredibly high .51 percent. Death by alcohol poisoning usually occurs at 0.35 percent or 0.40 percent. Ivy's death was ruled an accident. An alcoholic drinking herself to death seemed reasonable to the police. This same justification was used for many of the murders that Jordan committed. It is a testament to Jordan's intelligence that he targeted only alcoholics, giving him an alibi for each murder he committed. This negligence is also a major fault of statistics-based policing. Stats-based policing essentially involves providing the most favourable stats possible in order to get the most money possible out of the federal budget. Hence, police in the city in which Jordan was operating might have been reluctant to call the murders of these women what they were as it would have negatively impacted the city's stats.

Jordan lurked in the shadows for a few years after Ivy's death, but he didn't completely stay out of trouble. A few drunk driving charges and charges for performing lewd acts in public places kept him busy. Then in 1974, he was back in prison for indecent sexual assault. He was only sentenced to two years for the crime; however, he didn't even serve much of that short sentence. In 1975, Jordan was back out. He kidnapped a mentally impaired woman from a mental institution and raped her. Again he was only sentenced to 26 months for this crime.

Jordan financed his alcohol addiction and legal defences by speculating on the stock market. While not wealthy, he was very smart, or lucky, at where he invested his money.

When Jordan got out of prison the next time, he opened a barber shop near the DTES. It wasn't so much a place of business as a place to lure women to drink with him. For the next few years, he targeted Indigenous women specifically. Three Indigenous women died right in his shop - Mary Johns on July 30, 1982, with a blood alcohol level of .76 percent; Patricia Thomas on December 15, 1984, with a blood alcohol level of .51 percent; and Patricia Andrew on June 28, 1985, with a blood alcohol level of .79 percent. Also at nearby hotels, three more Indigenous women died while drinking in his company: Mary Johnson on November 30, 1980, with a blood alcohol level of .34 percent; Barbara Paul on September 11, 1981, with a blood alcohol level of .41 percent; and Vera Harry on November 19, 1986[91]. Jordan was never arrested or charged with any of these deaths. He was very smart to report the deaths to police to avert suspicion. As far as the police were concerned, they were alcoholics and prostitutes and at high risk for such a fate anyway. The coroner ruled all the deaths as accidental.

1987 was the year in which he killed Vanessa Lee Buckner. He was seen entering the hotel room with her and also left the room several times during the night to get more alcohol. At six in the morning, he left for the last time. An hour or so later, law enforcement officials received an anonymous call stating where they could find the body of a young prostitute. Vanessa Lee Buckner had a staggering blood alcohol level of .91 percent. Jordan was not charged, but finally his being around when so many women died aroused some suspicion. He was put under police surveillance. Police kept watch on Jordan from the 12th of October to the 26th of November. During this time, they watched as he stalked the red light districts of Vancouver, paying special attention to Indigenous street workers. On the 20th of November, he found a new victim, Rosemary Wilson, and took her to the Balmoral Hotel. Fortunately, police were able to prevent her death by intervening in time. They didn't step in too soon, though, since her blood alcohol level was clocked at .52 percent. In that week alone, they prevented Jordan from killing three other Indigenous women, Verna Chartrand, who had a blood alcohol level of .43 percent, and Mabel Olson, both of whom were saved at the Pacific Hotel, and Sheila Joe who was saved at the Rainbow Hotel. The surveillance ended much too soon, however. On November 29, 1987, the naked body of Edna Shade was found dead at the Glenaird Hotel with a blood alcohol level of .77 percent. Fingerprints on the vodka bottle and glasses proved Jordan was there drinking with her. He was never charged with Edna's murder. But at least he was charged with Vanessa's and would make it to trial.

Jordan was convicted of the lesser charge of manslaughter rather than murder. He was sentenced to 15 years and on appeal it was reduced to nine. He only actually served six years. The serial killer targeting vulnerable Indigenous women was let out in 1994 to pick up where he left off. None of the other murders were ever properly tied to him in an effort to keep him in prison and off the streets. Seemed like no-one cared enough to follow through. He did, however, spend the rest of his life back in and out of prison for offences involving violations of his probation which required him to abstain completely from alcohol and to stay within a certain geographical area, both of which he failed to do on several occasions. Jordan died of cirrhosis on July 7, 2006. He was 75 years old.

All in all, Jordan's case practically proves the bias that prevents the proper classification and resolution of serial killers that target Indigenous women. There is no doubt that serial killers who specifically target Indigenous women and girls exist, but law enforcement authorities have proven to be notoriously inefficient when it comes to solving serial murder cases if the victims aren't young, white and pretty, essentially Ted Bundy's ideal victim type.

John Martin Crawford

"Ask anyone in Canada who John Martin Crawford is or who his victims were and you are likely to be greeted with a blank stare."[92] At the time of his arrest, Crawford was the second most deadly serial killer in Canadian history next to Clifford Olson. He was a serial killer who targeted Indigenous women in the provinces of Alberta and Saskatchewan in the 1980s and '90s. Crawford was convicted of murdering Mary Jane Serloin in Lethbridge, Alberta in 1981 when he was just 19 years old. The manslaughter conviction he agreed to plead guilty to meant that he served less than a decade in prison for her murder. Upon his release, he picked up where he left off with a vengeance, leaving a trail of rape and murder behind him. In just one year, he raped and killed 16-year-old Shelley Napope, 30-year-old Eva Taysup, and 22-year-old Calinda Waterhen. All three remained on Saskatchewan's Missing Persons List until their remains were found two years after they disappeared. Police knew almost immediately it was John Crawford, and he was ultimately convicted and sent to prison in 1996. He is currently serving three concurrent life sentences in the Saskatchewan Penitentiary in Prince Albert.

Crawford was suspected of committing other murders and rapes during that time period as well, but not enough evidence could be found to bring him to justice in those cases. The remains of 38-year-old Janet Sylvestre, who Crawford was charged of raping two years prior, was found in a grove of trees in Saskatoon in October 13, 1994; 25-year-old Shirley Lonethunder from Saskatoon went missing on December 24, 1991, while Christmas shopping; and Cynthia Baldhead ominously disappeared from her Indigenous community as well around that time. Three other Indigenous women came forward after his arrest was made public with tales of how Crawford choked and raped them around the same time as the murders in 1992. No charges were brought against him for these crimes.

So why do so few people know of John Crawford? At the same time of his trial in 1996, all of Canada was fixated on the trial of Paul Bernardo and Karla Homolka in Toronto. It was painfully obvious that the *Ken and Barbie Killers* were much more newsworthy than Crawford killing a lot of Indigenous women who worked in the sex trade. When questioned about the media's lack of news coverage of this lethal serial killer, their excuse was that it lacked compelling drama. In their opinion, the accusation of racism was unfounded. Yet, as journalist Warren Goulding so accurately pointed out in his scathing account of Canada's apathy in the murders of Indigenous women, *Just Another Indian: A Serial Killer and Canada's Indifference*, "There was an abundance of sex. There was murder and mutilation. There was a depraved, slack-jawed predator supported at every turn by his devoted mother. There was an unscrupulous informer who earned more than $15,000 for his efforts to trap Crawford and, in the process, avoided being named as a co-accused in at least one of the murders at which he had been present. Finally, there was a world-renowned forensic anthropologist who, with a handful of bones and a dearth of evidence, eventually brought a serial killer to trial. It sounds like a fairly compelling drama by any standards. And yet, most members of the general public don't even recognize the name of John Martin Crawford."[93]

Everything we know about Crawford's background indicates that he was a 'textbook' serial killer: white male, family history of alcoholism, sexual abuse at age 4 and again at age 7 at the hands of babysitters, history of suicide attempts, an attraction to fire that left him with burn scars on his upper chest, neck and arms, overprotective and domineering mother, and more. He displayed early signs of mental instability by talking to inanimate objects and hearing voices he later said tormented him. Crawford also showed serious signs of sexual deviance or, some might say, early onset of sexual maturity. At the age of 13, along with several of his friends, Crawford paid an 11-year-old girl to have sex with them. He was also very young when he first started abusing different substances. He first became addicted to sniffing glue at age 12 but quickly escalated to drinking and taking either street or prescription drugs. He admitted to counsellors later that he started to hear voices when he turned 16. At 19, Crawford committed his first murder.

Mary Jane Serloin, a 35-year-old Peigan woman from the town of Brocket in the Northern Piikani Nation in Alberta, met John Crawford at a Lethbridge beverage room called the Bridge on December 23, 1981. Both were drinking heavily and seemed to bond over drinks. They left together around 10:00 pm. When he returned at midnight, he was alone. The next morning Mary Jane was found naked and battered in an alcove behind the nearby fire hall. She had been beaten to death and was abandoned, the signs of violent sexual violation clear upon her person. Bite marks were clearly visible on the victim's neck and breasts. Crawford was promptly connected to the crime, arrested and charged with murder in the first degree. The police were sure they had the right guy given the "unique dental profile of the bite marks. They were a match to Crawford's cast." [94] Despite this compelling evidence, a plea bargain was deemed necessary and Crawford agreed to plead guilty to the lesser charge of manslaughter. The judge sentenced him to ten years in prison, the maximum allowable. "Justice L.D. MacLean said that one of the most troubling aspects of the attack was Crawford's callous disregard for what had just happened, returning, as he did, to the tavern for beer and pizza minutes after taking the life of Mary Jane Serloin." [95] For Mary Jane's family, the news of her death was hard to bear. But almost as bad was the fact that no-one seemed to care. With a couple of cursory mentions in the local newspaper, it practically went unnoticed. Contact with police was scarce. According to Justine English, Mary Jane's sister, "they (the police) didn't even have the decency to let me know what was going on. I really would have wanted to see him, to see what the guy that killed my sister looked like."[96]

Despite the violent nature of the crime, Crawford was first released in September 1987 after serving only five years. Within months, he was back inside for parole violation and wasn't released again until March 1989.

Following his release from prison, Crawford moved in with his mother. At some point during his incarceration, Crawford was transferred to a prison in Saskatchewan, and his mother moved to Saskatoon from Alberta to be closer to him. It was in this penitentiary where he met and befriended a fellow inmate and career criminal by the name of Bill Corrigan who was serving ten years for armed robbery. Crawford emerged from prison ready to get back to his old ways and didn't waste much time. Drinking and using hard drugs, Crawford, and later Corrigan when he was released in 1991, would often drive around in an inebriated state stalking the red light districts of the city looking for prostitutes. Crawford was arrested in 1990 for trying to pick up a prostitute who turned out to be an undercover cop and fined $250. He was known as a 'bad trick' among sex trade workers.

1992 saw John Crawford on a rapid downward spiral. Fueled more and more by any pill he could get his hands on, his latest favourite was Ritalin, a drug prescribed to treat ADHD in children or teens. On May 9, 1992, Janet Sylvestre, a Dene woman from La Loche in northern Saskatchewan, who was commonly known as Smiley, informed police that John

Crawford had raped her across from the men's group home his mother operated. Police apprehended him fairly quickly, finding him drunk and passed out on a beach suffering from sunstroke. He was charged and held in remand for a month, but when Janet didn't show up for court, the charge was stayed. Crawford's mother posted $4,000 bail and he was released in her care. Two years later, on October 12, 1994, Janet disappeared after leaving a bar with a man around midnight. Her body was found the next day by an elderly man out for his morning walk along a gravel road 15 kilometres outside Saskatoon. Naked and with a plastic bag over her head, she was asphyxiated.[97] Incredibly, law enforcement was unable to find any forensic evidence that it was Crawford who murdered Janet. Even though they suspected it was he given his personal motive and opportunity. Janet's murder is still listed as unsolved.

Two other women later came forward with stories that Crawford also picked them up that summer, choked and raped them, and threatened them with worse. In September, Shelley Napope made the mistake of stopping to chat with Crawford, whom she had met on one other occasion, and his sidekick Bill Corrigan. They were going about their usual routine of cruising around looking to pick up women and drinking when they saw Shelley. Outgoing and gregarious, Shelley asked the men for a ride to a friend's house. They agreed, but on the way back, Crawford detoured out of the city limits and towards the more rural and isolated spot of Moon Lake. According to the later testimony of Bill Corrigan, there Crawford raped, beat and stabbed Shelley to death. Out of fear for his own life, Corrigan testified that he helped dispose of her body by covering it with leaves. On September 20, Crawford abducted, raped and strangled Eva Taysup. The very next day, he did the same thing to Calinda Waterhen. His MO changed by actually wrapping Eva and Calinda in blankets and burying their bodies. October 1992 and most of 1993 saw him back in prison for the brutal beating of a man over a cigarette. John Crawford was completely unhinged.

Always one to make an easy buck, Bill Corrigan decided to become a paid informant for the RCMP. In July 1993, he decided to make a few bucks by snitching on Crawford. He told his handler all about how he witnessed Crawford brutally rape, beat and stab a girl named 'Angie' (who was actually Shelley Napope) to death in September 1992 and dispose of her body out by Moon Lake. He also said that he wouldn't be surprised if there were more bodies there as well. They made several attempts to find the exact spot where 'Angie' was left, but to no avail. They could not find her remains. They remained hidden until October 1, 1994, when Brian Reichert stumbled across a skull while looking for deer with a friend and reported it to police.

Later in October, a second set of skeletal remains was found close to where the first set was – close enough that law enforcement officials started to suspect they had found a dumping site for a serial killer. Shortly after expanding their search grid, a third set was found. So by the end the month, they had four dead people. The only one they could identify for sure was Janet Sylvestre.

Law enforcement knew pretty much within a week after the remains were found that John Crawford was whom they were looking for, thanks to Corrigan and the information he had provided about the murder the previous year. Now they just had to identify the three other sets of remains and build a murder case against him. First they needed to keep an eye on Crawford and find Corrigan.

Crawford was still out prowling and doing what he did. On October 11, he picked up Theresa Kematch. After driving her to a secluded spot, he proceeded to rape, beat and violate her. However, this time he didn't kill her. He just tossed her out of his car and drove off. Unbelievably, that night was the first night that he was under police surveillance. The police saw him pick her up and drive to a secluded location. They followed. From a mere three meters away, the rape and assault on Theresa took place. The police later stated that they didn't realize she was in any danger. They admitted that they didn't want to blow their cover and risk Crawford taking off; however, if they thought she was in any real danger, they would have stepped in. What the police did do is come scrape poor Theresa off the pavement, all battered and bruised, but instead of taking her to a hospital, they arrested her and locked her in a cell all night. The next morning they released her and drove her to her parent's house.

When law enforcement tracked down Bill Corrigan to be a witness for their case, they found him on the lam for stealing a small amount of money from his landlord. They agreed to pay that back for him and talk the landlord out of pressing charges, and give him $15,000 if he could get Crawford to confess to the murders on tape and then testify at the trial. Which, of course, he did. Crawford did confess to the murders of Eva, Shelley and Calinda; however, he adamantly denied killing Janet Sylvestre.

Invisible Victims

Crawford was finally arrested in January 1995 for the murders of Eva Taysup, Shelley Napope and Calinda Waterhen without much fanfare. He was convicted in May 1996 of second degree murder in the case of Eva and Calinda, and first degree murder of Shelley. He was sentenced to three life terms to be served concurrently with no chance of parole.

John Crawford murdered women, including a 16-year-old girl, in the worst way possible. From Bill Corrigan's testimony, we heard some of the details surrounding Shelley's death. From forensic anthropologist, Dr. Ernie Walker, we heard some of the details of what Eva endured before her death. And from the testimony of Theresa and the other women who came forward, we know a little more about the brutal nature of Crawford. However, all of the horrors these women suffered will never be fully known. Too much time had passed before they were found for the cause of death to be proven by forensic evidence. Still today, there are other Indigenous women missing from that area including Shirley Lonethunder and Cynthia Baldhead, and murders that are unsolved including Janet Sylvestre.

So what do you think? Compelling drama or not? There are many reasons why the case of John Crawford is not deemed newsworthy. Race and social standing of the victims are among the forerunners. When we as a society can relate to the victims, we seem to have more empathy for them. We need to ask ourselves, why do we find it so hard to relate to Indigenous women?

"During the course of the Crawford trial, women and elders wore blankets to signify solidarity as a people in the face of indifference. Just as some of the victims were wrapped in blankets and laid in the brush where they died, the elders and women reclaimed that as a symbol of healing and togetherness."[98]

Bobby Fowler

Bobby Jack Fowler was a career criminal originally from Texas, USA. He died in a Newport, Oregon, prison in 2006 from lung cancer at the age of 66 while serving a 16-year sentence for kidnapping, attempted rape and assault. After a sample of his DNA was obtained in Canada, it was confirmed that he was responsible for the death of at least one teenager who had disappeared on BC's Highway of Tears, and was a strong suspect in the murders of Pamela Darlington and Gale Weys as well.

Born in 1939, Fowler was a transient worker drifting from town to town picking up odd jobs as he needed. An alcoholic and drug user, he was known to be violent but could also be charming when he wanted to be. RCMP Inspector Gary Shinkaruk stated for the *Vancouver Sun* that "he (Fowler) was of the belief that a lot of the women he came into contact with, specifically women that hitchhike and women that went to taverns and beer parlours and drank, that they had a desire to be sexually assaulted."[99] Fowler had made quite a career out of crime with convictions in several

US states and records for attempted murder, assault, arson and sexual assault.

In 2012, RCMP task force, E-PANA, that investigated the Highway of Tears murders, asked for DNA found on Colleen Macmillan's remains from 1974 to be retested. Tests conducted in 2007 could not find a match; however, progress is always being made in the area of forensic science. This time the DNA tests found a match once submitted to Interpol for comparison. The DNA belonged to Bobby Jack Fowler, who happened to be working for a roofing company in Prince George, BC in 1974. Unfortunately, Fowler was already deceased by that time and couldn't be convicted. However, the family was very grateful to finally know for sure what happened to Colleen.

Invisible Victims

Katherine McCarthy

Conclusion

Violence towards Indigenous women in Canada is escalating at alarming rates even though the country's overall crime rates are dropping and are at their lowest in over 40 years. Indigenous women are six times more likely to die a violent death and seven times more likely to be killed by a serial killer than non-Indigenous women. Indigenous women are also disproportionately represented in the homicide statistics. While making up only 4% of Canada's population, Indigenous women account for 16% of the females who are murdered.

With respect to the true number of MMIWs in Canada, no-one can say yet. The RCMP's data that was widely reported in the media has serious validity issues. Missing data from two large provinces with a high number of Indigenous people, missing information from information system backlogs, failure in capturing vital information on victims or missing persons, and an overall intrinsic motivation to skew the numbers towards family violence to conclude the crisis in an

Indigenous problem, all lead to doubts about the accuracy of the reported number. Grassroots organizations put the number somewhere around 4,000. The national inquiry that is due to kick off in the next few months will be able to identify and quantify the true number.

This state of affairs and MMIW crisis is still unknown to many people in Canada. One reason is the fact that for decades the media has deemed the deaths or disappearances of Indigenous women and girls as unnewsworthy. The media has the ability to not just inform, but to persuade society in general that we can make a difference. This is not to suggest that Canada's mainstream media come up with solutions for this problem, because only Indigenous people themselves know what they need to heal. But the media can absolutely play a role in supporting Indigenous people. Some effort is beginning to be made with the CBC, *Globe and Mail* and *Toronto Star;* however, much more can be done with how these cases are reported. Again this is where the national inquiry should provide recommendations.

The reason why this crisis is happening is complex. In the past couple of centuries, Indigenous women have been harmed in many ways. Colonialization has disassociated women from everything they valued: their communities, land, family, culture, spirituality and sense of self. But Indigenous women are strong. Mentally and spiritually. And very resilient. A hundred years ago, Duncan Campbell Scott vehemently stated that he would not stop until all the "Indians" were gone. Well, despite everything, we're still here. Only 1.4 million of us, but the fact that we still exist speaks volumes.

Invisible Victims

Acknowledgments

Thank you to my editor, proof-readers, and cover artist for your support:
Katherine

Aeternum Designs (book cover), Bettye McKee (editor), Dr. Peter Vronsky (editor), Dr. RJ Parker, VP Publications, Lorrie Suzanne Phillippe, Marlene Fabregas, Darlene Horn, Ron Steed, Robyn MacEachern, Lee Knieper Husemann, Kathi Garcia, Vicky Matson-Carruth, Linda H. Bergeron

Invisible Victims

Crimes Canada Collection

An exciting 24-volume series collection, edited by crime historian Dr. Peter Vronsky and true crime author and publisher Dr. RJ Parker.

VOLUMES:

(URL LINK ON NEXT PAGE)

1. Robert Pickton: The Pig Farmer Killer by C.L. Swinney

Invisible Victims

2. Marc Lepine: The Montreal Massacre by RJ Parker
3. Paul Bernardo and Karla Homolka by Peter Vronsky
4. Shirley Turner: Doctor, Stalker, Murderer by Kelly Banaski
5. Canadian Psycho: Luka Magnotta by Cara Lee Carter
6. The Country Boy Killer: Cody Legebokoff by JT Hunter
7. The Killer Handyman by C.L. Swinney
8. Hell's Angels Biker Wars by RJ Parker
9. The Dark Strangler by Michael Newton
10. The Alcohol Murders by Harriet Fox
11. Peter Woodcock: Canada's Youngest Serial Killer by Mark Bourrie
12. Clifford Olson: The Beast of British Columbia by Elizabeth Broderick
13. Taking Tori by Kelly Banaski
14. Bandits and Renegades by Ed Butts

View these and future books in this collection at:

rjpp.ca/CC-CRIMES-CANADA-BOOKS

Katherine McCarthy

About The Author

Katherine is a writer, graphic designer and book review blogger and of Mi'kmaq and Irish descent.

Following her heart, Katherine left a 20-year commerce and project management career to find a place in the Indie Writing industry. She is currently managing a graphic design company, *Aeternum Designs*, specializing in book cover art and promotional materials for independent authors. The Crime Cove Book Review Blog is where she discovered writing and reading about true crime is her passion.

Both an introvert and extrovert by nature, Katherine is comfortable at home surrounded by lots of books and quiet reflection, or being friendly and approachable out among the masses. To receive alerts of Katherine's upcoming releases and special offers, please sign up to her mailing list and follow along on her social media sites.

Website:
www.katherinemccarthy.com

Facebook: https://www.facebook.com/Katherine-McCarthy-Writer-1692052331016630/

Twitter:
https://twitter.com/KatMcCarthyTC

Google+:
https://plus.google.com/u/1/+KatherineMcCarthyAuthor/about

Email:
katmccarthywriter@gmail.com

Katherine McCarthy

Sources

1. http://www.aadnc-aandc.gc.ca/eng/1449240606362/1449240634871
2. http://www.theglobeandmail.com/news/national/aboriginals-six-times-more-likely-to-be-homicide-victims-statscan/article27475106/
3. http://www.statcan.gc.ca/tables-tableaux/sum-som/l01/cst01/legal12a-eng.htm
4. http://www.statcan.gc.ca/pub/11-630-x/11-630-x2015001-eng.htm
5. http://www.cbc.ca/news/politics/full-text-of-peter-mansbridge-s-interview-with-stephen-harper-1.2876934
6. http://www.amnesty.ca/sites/amnesty/files/amr200032004enstolensisters.pdf
7. http://www.theglobeandmail.com/news/politics/un-human-rights-investigator-says-canada-needs-inquiry-into-missing-aboriginal-women/article14870214/
8. https://www.hrw.org/report/2013/02/13/those-who-take-us-away/abusive-policing-and-failures-protection-Indigenous-women
9. http://www.oas.org/en/iachr/reports/pdfs/Indigenous-Women-BC-Canada-en.pdf
10. https://www.hrw.org/report/2013/02/13/those-who-take-us-away/abusive-policing-and-failures-protection-Indigenous-women

11. http://learningcircle.ubc.ca/files/2013/08/IRS-Colonialism-History-Impacts-2013.pdf
12. http://www.theglobeandmail.com/news/national/the-death-and-life-of-cindy-gladue/article24455472/
13. http://halifax.mediacoop.ca/story/we-didnt-think-time-images-would-be-painful-and-up/33782
14. https://ipsmo.files.wordpress.com/2010/12/newsworthy-victims-gilchrist-2010-missing-murdered-aboriginal-women.pdf
15. NWAC, Violations of Indigenous Human Rights Report, December 2002, pp. 4-5.
16. http://www.rcmp-grc.gc.ca/pubs/mmaw-faapd-eng.pdf
17. http://www.rcmp-grc.gc.ca/pubs/abo-aut/mmaw-fada-eng.htm
18. http://www.theglobeandmail.com/news/politics/70-per-cent-of-murdered-aboriginal-women-killed-by-Indigenous-men-rcmp-confirms/article23868927/
19. https://www.thestar.com/news/canada/2015/12/04/nearly-half-of-murdered-Indigenous-women-did-not-know-killers-star-analysis-shows.html
20. http://www.leaf.ca/wp-content/uploads/2015/06/2015-06-16-MMIW-LSC-2014-Fact-Sheet-final-version.pdf
21. http://www.rcmp-grc.gc.ca/pubs/abo-aut/mmaw-fada-eng.htm

22. https://www12.statcan.gc.ca/nhs-enm/2011/as-sa/99-011-x/2011001/tbl/tbl02-eng.cfm
23. http://www.ajic.mb.ca/volumel/chapter13.html
24. http://www.ajic.mb.ca/volumel/chapter13.html
25. Final Report Truth and Reconciliation Commission of Canada, Volume One:Summary, p.45
26. http://www.rcinet.ca/english/archives/column/the-link-africa/TruthandReconciliationCanadaSouthAfricaResidentialSchoolsAbuses/
27. Final Report of the Truth and Reconciliation Commission of Canada, Volume 1: Summary, p 3.
28. http://www.ictinc.ca/blog/indian-act-and-the-pass-system
29. http://www.ictinc.ca/blog/indian-act-and-the-permit-system-
30. http://learningcircle.ubc.ca/files/2013/08/IRS-Colonialism-History-Impacts-2013.pdf
31. http://Indigenousfoundations.arts.ubc.ca/home/government-policy/the-indian-act.html
32. http://www.nfb.ca/film/we_were_children/trailer/we_were_children_trailer/
33. Final Report Truth and Reconciliation Commission of Canada, Volume One: Summary, p. 106.

34. http://www.cbc.ca/news/canada/montreal/real-talk-on-race-sixties-scoop-not-recognized-1.3494343

35. http://Indigenousfoundations.arts.ubc.ca/home/government-policy/sixties-scoop.html

36. https://en.wikipedia.org/wiki/Compulsory_sterilization_in_Canada

37. http://historyofrights.ca/encyclopaedia/main-events/eugenics/

38. http://guides.library.utoronto.ca/c.php?g=251685&p=1675126

39. http://historyofrights.ca/encyclopaedia/main-events/eugenics/

40. https://intercontinentalcry.org/canadas-coerced-sterilization-of-first-nations-women/

41. Stote, Karen Dr., An Act of Genocide: Colonialism and the Sterilization of Aboriginal Women

42. Stote, Karen Dr. An Act of Genocide

43. http://news.nationalpost.com/news/canada/saskatoon-health-region-apologizes-after-aboriginal-women-felt-pressured-by-staff-to-have-tubes-tied

44. http://soulsurfing.website/2015/10/13/scientists-have-found-that-memories-may-be-passed-down-through-generations-in-our-dna/

45. http://discovermagazine.com/2013/may/13-grandmas-experiences-leave-epigenetic-mark-on-your-genes#.UqjR8dJDvng
46. https://beta.thestar.com/news/canada/2011/08/17/distraught_dad_fears_for_daughter_missing_in_saskatchewan.html
47. http://cjme.com/article/174528/body-found-near-herschel-identified-carol-king
48. https://soundcloud.com/vocm/mon-king2-lis
49. http://www.ctvnews.ca/cryptic-memorial-put-up-for-dead-woman-on-sask-property-1.743479
50. http://cjme.com/story/cryptic-messages-surround-carol-kings-death/37165
51. http://www.cbc.ca/news/canada/saskatchewan/dead-woman-s-ex-declares-innocence-1.1119924
52. http://www.cbc.ca/news/canada/saskatchewan/fire-at-king-home-not-the-first-rcmp-says-1.1092397
53. http://ckom.com/story/rcmp-yet-lay-charges-one-year-after-carol-king-disappearance/68615
54. http://globalnews.ca/news/1494929/feeling-of-safety-returns-to-herschel-sk-3-years-after-carol-king-homicide/
55. http://www.thewesternstar.com/News/Local/2015-08-06/article-4237175/Carol-King%26rsquo%3Bs-family-still-coping-with-her-loss/1

56. http://globalnews.ca/news/2153016/no-new-leads-in-carol-king-homicide/
57. http://rabble.ca/blogs/bloggers/krystalline-kraus/2013/05/activist-communique-seeking-justice-cheyenne-fox-0
58. https://www.thestar.com/news/gta/2014/01/19/the_police_say_suicide_the_family_says_murder.html
59. https://tworowtimes.com/news/national/family-cheyenne-fox-seek-justice/
60. http://aptn.ca/news/2014/09/13/family-of-deceased-Indigenous-woman-suing-toronto-police-for-14-million/
61. http://www.torontosun.com/2015/06/19/father-searches-for-answers-about-native-womans-death-in-toronto
62. http://aptn.ca/news/2013/05/15/first-nations-woman-killed-by-train-in-toronto-was-a-witness-in-murder-trial/
63. http://aptn.ca/news/2014/12/23/sudden-death-Indigenous-woman-left-family-without-justice/
64. http://rabble.ca/blogs/bloggers/johnbon/2013/06/homeless-deaths-mounting-record-pace-toronto
65. http://invisiblepeople.tv/blog/2011/09/terra-homeless-toronto-canada/
66. http://www.itstartswithus-mmiw.com/bella
67. http://www.itstartswithus-mmiw.com/bella

68. http://www.vancouversun.com/news/Police+reveal+details+Pana+investigation+into+female+unsolved+cases+northern/2331959/story.html

69. http://www.vancouversun.com/news/Video+RCMP+believe+there+more+than+Highway+Tears+killer/7296937/story.html

70. http://www.cbc.ca/missingandmurdered/mmiw/profile/tamara-lynn-chipman

71. http://www.cbc.ca/missingandmurdered/mmiw/profile/aielah-saric-auger

72. http://www.cbc.ca/player/play/1314202899

73. http://www.nytimes.com/2014/04/27/magazine/who-killed-anna-mae.html?_r=1

74. http://www.jfamr.org/doc/kmtest1.html

75. http://www.indiancountrynews.com/index.php/investigations/annie-mae-pictou-aquash/12087-looking-cloud-has-sentence-reduced-in-aquash-murder-case

76. http://www.indiancountrynews.com/index.php/investigations/annie-mae-pictou-aquash/12256-canadian-appeals-conviction-in-75-aim-slaying

77. http://www.jfamr.org/doc/banks.html

78. http://www.theglobeandmail.com/news/national/pri

me-targets-serial-killers-and-Indigenous-women/article27435090/

79. http://www.theglobeandmail.com/news/national/prime-targets-serial-killers-and-Indigenous-women/article27435090/

80. Swinney, Chris, The Pig Farmer Killer: Robert Pickton, pp. 33-34.

81. http://www.princegeorgecitizen.com/news/legebokoff-trial/legebokoff-had-system-to-murder-women-jury-told-1.1340317

82. Parker, RJ, (2015). Serial Killers Case Files, Third edition, USA

83. http://www.princegeorgecitizen.com/news/local-news/little-peace-for-families-of-legebokoff-s-victims-1.1698221

84. http://www.princegeorgecitizen.com/news/legebokoff-trial/judge-sentences-legebokoff-to-life-for-four-murders-1.1375816

85. http://www.princegeorgecitizen.com/news/legebokoff-trial/emotions-run-high-at-legebokoff-trial-1.1255252

86. http://www.pgfreepress.com/victim-impact-statements-given-in-court/

87. http://www.vancouversun.com/news/Families+Lege

bokoff+victims+give+emotional+statements+sentencing+hearing/10200243/story.html
88. http://www.globalpost.com/dispatch/news/regions/americas/canada/110615/canada-legalize-prostitution
89. https://www.amazon.com/Robert-Pickton-Farmer-Serial-Shocked-ebook/dp/B00TO141LA?ie=UTF8&qid=1463510048&ref_=tmm_kin_swatch_0&sr=8-1
90. https://www.amazon.com/Alcohol-Murders-Serial-Gilbert-Shocked-ebook/dp/B018Y9QF4I?ie=UTF8&qid=1463796854&ref_=tmm_kin_swatch_0&sr=8-1
91. http://murderpedia.org/male.J/j/jordan-gilbert-paul.htm
92. Goulding, Warren. Just Another Indian: A Serial Killer and Canada's Indifference, p. 210.
93. Goulding, Just Another Indian p. xvii.
94. Mellor, Lee. Cold North Killers: Canadian Serial Murder, p. 126.
95. Goulding, Just Another Indian p. 74.
96. Goulding, Just Another Indian p. 75.
97. Goulding, Just Another Indian p. 136.
98. http://bruntmag.com/issue3/give-her-a-face.html
99. http://www.vancouversun.com/news/Video+RCMP+believe+there+more+than+Highway+Tears+killer/7296937/story.html

Made in the USA
Columbia, SC
07 November 2017